I CHING
of LOVE

CW01457135

LO SCARABEO

THE I CHING OF LOVE

Artwork by Ma Nishavdo
Text by Swami Anand Videha
Translations by Studio RGE, Avvalon
Printed by Wai Man Book Binding

© Lo Scarabeo 2020
All rights reserved

Lo Scarabeo
Via Cigna 110
10155 Torino – Italy
info@loscarabeo.com
www.loscarabeo.com

Follow *Lo Scarabeo Tarot*
on Facebook and Instagram

TABLE OF CONTENTS

THE I CHING
OF LOVE

The Book of Changes or *I Ching* is the founding work of Chinese thought. It is a written work that dates back to a legendary era, and was subsequently structured over time. The basic text, now widespread, dates back to about 3,000 years ago, but over the centuries that followed, it had distinguished editors who enriched it, including Confucius and great Taoist Masters who strengthened its framework by making the *Void* key as they considered it the Origin of all existence.

The *I Ching* bases its entire oracular vision on a scientific understanding of the laws of the universe, which unties its essential core from particular traditional or cultural affiliations; and awakens to a truth on which the whole of existence rests: *life is eternal change.*

This is the only certainty we have! Understanding it allows us to tune in organically to the primordial breath that perpetually regenerates and recreates the entire cosmos and, therefore, each of us as well.

In reality, however unconsciously we do so, we participate in this continuous creation: in the incessant flow of day into night, in the changing of summer into autumn and then into winter to flourish into spring, in the progress of our life towards death, we participate in that hidden harmony, the result of the interaction of two factors or primordial breaths - the *yin*, the feminine principle and the *yang,* the masculine principle - on whose dance the entire cosmos and all our existence depends. Not only that: tuning into that flow allows us to perceive the universal source and vibrate in unison with that cosmic harmony, towards which every being is moving.

It is an overview that is based on the observation of the laws and forces that govern the cosmos and nature, and consequently also man and his social and existential frameworks, codified in 64 hexagrams whose intent is to suggest individual steps to direct action towards a communion with the mystery of the universe. But it is good to remember that these judgements do not give norms or commandments, they are suggestions that each one must decode according to his or her own situation. The use of the *I Ching* therefore calls for an intuitive approach that has nothing to do with common logical understanding, as Jung has pointed out.

Given these presuppositions, the love we are talking about here is nothing more than the manifestation of that primordial breath when it operates as a force of cohesion, in all its forms. An energy of which we are a living testimony, as it is the result of the union of two people who have intertwined their primary breaths, uniting themselves carnally and in this way merging with the essence from which everything originates.

Our living in time, troubled by so many worries, burdened with so many priorities, overwhelmed by commitments, responsibilities and stimuli leads to a loss of that organic vision that still lingers in us. This is confirmed by our primary aspiration to be happy, no matter how confused and distorted our quest for it may be. And the many traditions of Truth, which have always existed, without geographical or historical distinctions, testify to the deep need we all have for harmony, something that allows us to solve the enigma that we otherwise are. And it is precisely in the answer to the question: "who am I?" realized in an experiential way, that the much desired peace and quiet will be achieved.

The I Ching of Love accompanies self-knowledge, without wanting to deny or replace individual responsibility in this quest. In fact, nothing theoretical can replace the experience that leads, by degrees and errors, to being oneself. The idea of divination that underlies these cards does not presuppose any reading of the future: they are existential suggestions that allow us to see what we are in the moment, so as to understand what is happening with objectivity. The invitation is to activate one's own inner laboratory where one can analyze oneself, without denying or judging anything of what one is, but living every characteristic of one's being without repressing oneself.

It may be difficult, given the many hardships of civilization and the conditioning suffered. On the other hand, beginning with sexuality, only by living it with totality it is possible to experience that point of transcendence in which lovers merge and unite themselves to the primordial breath, experiencing an intimate communion with the cosmos and its primordial principle. But before reaching that orgasmic peak, there are many aspects of us that ask to be experienced and resolved: for example, the sense of emptiness or feeling alone that may have pushed us into the arms of a lover; and that constantly urge us to fill our lives with something - people, objects, stimuli of all kinds, now even virtual - in order to silence them.

A sincere search for the Truth requires us to get naked in front of ourselves, living the whole of our moods, fears and dynamics as they characterize us, inhibiting or exalting us. The observation will help us to see what brings joy and pain, so as to understand, step by step, how to direct our lives towards intimate harmony.

The Oracle is precious in that it solicits insights that can activate a process of transformation that otherwise would be lost in our habitual compulsion to just repeat what generates discomfort and frustration. A constant and sincere use of these cards will allow us to approach what happens to us with more detachment, adding to the common reactions a transcendent point of view, something that gives a clearer view of the whole. And it is precisely the experience lived that will give tangibility to those understandings.

The first step of this adventure can only be this: to love oneself in a sincere and unconditional way; in fact, only a total acceptance of oneself makes it possible to really know oneself. And however long it may seem, one should live for a year simply trying to love oneself; using this time to observe and describe oneself, perhaps keeping a diary in which to tell what one is, in all the aspects that gradually emerge, without excluding anything.

The important thing is to observe and write down, without judging or altering anything, using the deck of cards to better understand the mechanics of one's actions. It may come as a surprise but detached observation and acceptance will make it possible to dissolve what torments us, resolving the deep conflict with ourselves that usually undermines our integrity and weakens us.

It is important to remember that the use of these cards does not involve any knowledge of or belonging to Chinese culture. It is simply a matter of activating one's perceptive faculties, starting from the introspective spark that we all have. From this point of view, the experience of love, with all the dynamics that accompany it, is a key experience to access, turn on and illuminate the whole of our being and in particular, parts of us that perhaps we never even wanted to see.

Falling in love is in itself a sinking into one's own being, which overwhelms every balance and leaves naked, without certainties, literally at the mercy of another human being. It is quite likely that most readers find themselves living that all-encompassing experience, and perhaps they are looking for tools to manage dynamics, emotions, fears, indescribable joys, conflicts and sensations so vague as to be elusive. In this case, the support of these thousands of years old understandings can help to make that chaotic swirl a path of growth, towards the harmony that every love potentially brings with it.

Whatever the current state of the relationship, it is important to ask one's partner for space for the experiment that the use of these cards implies. Even better would be an active participation of both parties, but the process can also be carried out individually: if you face it as a whole, and the intent is sincere, any clarity achieved will also be reflected on the partner.

First of all, it is good to verify within oneself the existence of any resistance that prevents love from flowing. Without trying to change everyday life, observe how, why and at what times or situations do you back out, hold back something or react violently. Also in this case, it is good to keep a diary, and especially give yourself time to elaborate any understandings. The use of these cards will allow you to get suggestions for understanding and learning to respond, thus breaking the usual tendency to react, with all the ensuing repercussions.

To make that detached observation easier it is important to learn to relax the body, which can easily - especially in the most intimate moments - stiffen. The easiest way is to learn to make good use of exhalation.

When you feel that you are holding back and resisting, bring your attention to your breath and exhale immediately. You can also visualize venting all your tensions with those deep exhalations; repeat the exercise calmly, until you feel that the body is no longer contracted.

Don't underestimate the simplicity of this suggestion: many of those who have practiced it have managed, for example, to make love in a more relaxed way, touching orgasmic peaks never experienced before. Yet it is the clarity of vision that will benefit the most, giving mental openings previously unknown on the whole of the characteristics of love, otherwise invisible.

And precisely because observation is the cornerstone of any understanding, it is good to not take the idea of *knowing how to observe* for granted: from an introspective point of view, the use of sight is devoid of any intensity. In fact, it is totally functional to action, striving towards a conquest or a goal. Introspection, on the other hand, requires being receptive, embracing and *accepting* what one wants to perceive. In fact, the *I Ching* suggests a way to "feminine" knowledge, where understanding is achieved by letting oneself go to the flow of existence.

It is an unusual manner in today's predominant culture, and may require some effort to give space to a relaxed predisposition. On the other hand, if you decide to inhabit your inner dimension, it is essential to activate it. So try, at certain times of the day - and when it is possible even for a few days - to just sit back and let things happen by themselves. If you feel the need to focus on something, you can watch the sunrise or sunset, or look at a flower. Just look, without forcing your eyesight; on the contrary, try to withdraw your gaze a bit inside, so as to embrace the context in which the object of your observation is immersed.

Don't analyze, don't rationalize, don't say anything... simply observe, without any effort. Keep your eyes open, embrace that flower, that sunset, that dawn without any expectation. Little by little you will feel intimately connected, you will vibrate at the same frequency... and you may have the feeling that every distance fades: you and that flower are one! That very perception will lead you to see life with different eyes, from a different point of view.

In this experiment the important thing is *spontaneity*. Do not make an exercise or a method of it, otherwise you will feed your inclination to conquer, to control, to act. It is therefore better to constantly change the context: sometimes, you could simply do nothing, relax in a park and look at the sky. Or, you can simply close your eyes and observe what moves within you: thoughts, feelings, emotions, desires that come and go. Start to observe the dreamlike world in which you are immersed: this is a great start to getting closer to yourself. Do so without judging, without the pretense of modifying what you see: let everything happen by itself. Learn to be a simple observer, a witness.

Such moments of spontaneous meditation are more effective than the presumption to meditate regularly, either because time can be a tyrant, or because unconsciously there will be the presumption to obtain a result, for example: the conquest of one's being! Any realization has always taken place in a state of complete abandonment.

The sages who gave birth to the *I Ching* or who revived it over the centuries, have proven and taught that it is possible to participate in the harmony of the universe by tuning into its laws, letting go, or "acting without acting". The power of the Oracle is hidden in this aptitude and will be revealed in a space of stillness and calm.

So find moments when you allow yourself to disappear. Sitting comfortably in an armchair, or immersed in a corner in nature, try to perceive what the world is like, without you: free from your struggles, anger, depression... what is the world? Learn, even for a moment, not to be there; you can even do it at home. Without saying anything to any of your family members, observe what goes on...without participating. Sit in a chair, and let yourself go with the idea of not being there... observe how everything goes on, maybe a little more in peace, with less conflict. You will gain an understanding that will orient your introspective process in a different way. Surely, the intent of wanting to put things in order will vanish: you will see, with amazement, that they are already in order! And most probably the perception of a vibration, of a fragrance, of a sensation will begin to emerge, which could give you an idea of what led you to create and be a part of the family you are now living in. And here the idea itself will be perceived as something transcendent.

These meditations, done spontaneously, even for a brief moment - without a fixed framework and without specific schedules - can give surprising results: simply being aware that the world can go on very well without you, will put things in perspective and will lead you to rethink the sense of your existence. But above all, it will open you up to a receptivity that you may never have imagined, which will amplify the content of these oracular messages.

Another key factor that will enhance your introspective process is *cultivating the art of listening*. The whole *I Ching* is based on listening to the voice of existence, translated and encoded in ideograms that then gave a perception through images. And it was precisely this distinctive trait that allowed a network of correspondences to unfold between the transcendent aspect and our microcosm, avoiding the duplication that other forms of writing generate.

To reactivate that syntony and allow the Oracle to operate as a vehicle of harmony that underlies the entire expansion of the cosmos, we need to refine our auditory faculties, trying simple meditative devices that once again privilege spontaneity. Here they are, in brief, as summarized by Osho, a Master of Reality who dedicated his life to the awakening of awareness: "Now I will tell you the art of listening: walk about until exhausted or dance or do vigorous breathing and then, dropping to the ground, listen. Or, repeat your name loudly until exhausted and then suddenly stop and listen. Or, at the point of sleep when sleep has not yet come and external wakefulness vanishes, be alert and suddenly listen."

Through these simple strategies, a connection will be established with the universal truth that the sages heard and then shared. As all of them have done, we - the new entronauts - must abandon the verbal sphere and recreate a vibrational perception. This is not difficult, because in nature it continues to manifest itself: in the morning, for example, try to listen to the chirping of birds; and with time, refine your perception, listening to what the flowers or blades of grass are communicating. Soon you will reach the threshold of consciousness that allowed the first shamans to approach the oracular judgements contained in the *I Ching*, using the stems of the yarrow flower.

Remember that in order to "feel" it is not important what you listen to, but *the way* you listen: a receptive, passive listening, made with sincerity, purity and lightness of heart, brings you closer to the message that everyone would like to hear, and that in fact echoes everywhere in existence. Not hearing it depends on our not having activated - or rather having forgotten - the specific existential harmony that reveals it.

Strengthened by the understandings resulting from an introspective process, one can finally approach falling in love, love and the set of upheavals that always accompany it, living it as an opportunity to be reborn, to recreate oneself, to open oneself to dimensions and horizons otherwise unthinkable.

The responses to each consultation are never "forever". And the journey of love can never be exhausted in a single understanding. This deck of cards appears as a companion for life that you can consult from time to time, as the situation requires you to return to prepare to listen with the spirit of a witness who looks down from a hill: a simple, detached viewer who observes what happens.

Before any consultation it is important to give yourself time to calm down. You can do this by relaxing your breath for a few minutes. It is not necessary to relax the whole body, it is enough to focus on breathing and let the breath flow naturally: close your eyes and observe the air that comes in and out. Remember not to concentrate, because otherwise whatever happens around you will become a source of disturbance. The simple conscious presence that observes the breath as it enters and exits is enough!

This meditative strategy can also be used in everyday life, when something is disturbing. The simple relaxation of the breath and its quiet observation in which nothing is excluded, will allow you to incorporate the existence, without being overwhelmed: you can do it in the train, on the bus, in the car... without anyone noticing!

Once you have activated a state of conscious presence, it will be easy to approach the Oracle - even without asking specific questions - allowing you to receive the right message, in function with your experience of the moment. The testimonies received confirm that the constant use of the deck of cards allows you to grow and "rise in love", thus bringing falling in love to its full completion, otherwise predestined to be a victim of failure due to the many misfortunes that usually make it a net in which you feel trapped, eager finally only to escape.

Mix the deck and unfold it in front of you. Then turn a card with your left hand and focus on the drawing, being receptive to what it transmits to you. When you feel that you are set in the context generated by the card, read the judgement. Don't rush to interpret: let yourself be absorbed in that message, and let *it* activate *you*. In this way introspection will draw a new course for itself, generating a different development of things.

If you feel the need to experiment with specific meditative strategies, ones more responsive to your psychophysical balance, you may wish to visit the "meditate" section of www.osho.com. The methods proposed do not require any traditional membership and are non-denominational; as a whole they offer to contemporary man that "science of the soul" that underlies all the paths of research of the Truth.
In the section "online courses for meditating" it is possible to find precise suggestions for cultivating the art of observing, the art of listening and the art of relaxing: primary foundations of any introspective path.

SIMPLIFIED READING METHOD

Find a moment to be with yourself in a secluded environment, free from everyday stresses. Relax by simply observing your breath (see above) and, when you feel you can establish contact with your most intimate self, shuffle the cards: the 64 traditional hexagrams of the *Book of Changes* have been read with love in mind and translated into images that give an immediate impact. Visualize inwardly your current experience of love: let it emerge in front of you for what it is, do not judge it, do not interpret it, do not wish it different; it is not even necessary to verbalize a question. Remember: you are not looking for solace, nor do you wish to change what happens to you. When you feel ready, spread out the deck and, with your left hand, turn a card: read the description and contemplate the image, observing how it illuminates your state of affairs. Close your eyes and meditate silently on the message. Acceptance is the first key to reading these cards, capable of producing change, but above all capable of helping you to understand the experience that life is offering you... and remember: even this will pass, it is only one season of your life. Therefore, take what the card offers you, without beating yourself down or exalting yourself. This is the fundamental lesson of the *I Ching of Love*.

THE JUDGEMENTS

1. THE CREATIVE DESIRE

Eastern tradition sees desire as the beginning of the universe. This card is an invitation to not complicate life: *accept desire*. It is not good to fight against sexuality. Every repression will have you fighting against yourself... and to reach full realization you need all your strength. The card indicates that you are in tune with the creative power of the universe.

2. RECEPTIVITY

This card is a sign of a strong *Yin* presence, that is, receptivity, in your life. Observe how it governs you, what it implies and what comes from it: the creative force is settling and gaining concreteness in you.

3. THE INITIAL DIFFICULTY

The Oracle offers an invitation to not reduce your partner to an object, nor to sell oneself in the name of love, but to open oneself to the freedom where love can exist.

4. YOUTHFUL INEXPERIENCE

The Oracle is telling you that you are facing an abyss, but don't worry: by necessity, the carefreeness that characterizes this card leads you to flow, thus overcoming any obstacle that prevents you from progressing.

5. WAITING

In love it is important to let love itself be fulfilled. Waiting is a spell... For a moment you come in contact with who you are: you are completely centered in yourself. The Oracle says you are waiting. Don't wish for anything else!

6. CONFLICT

We often embellish love with dreams and fantasies, with presumptions and beliefs, preventing it from existing or conditioning it to the point of deforming it. Is this your case? Observe how you manipulated your love...

7. COHESION

In every reality of life, and especially in love, it is good to have a fulcrum of cohesion in oneself, so any encounter will be shared and you can enrich and expand in contact with each other. Refocus on yourself!

8. COMPLEMENTARITIES' SOLIDARITY

The Tao, to manifest itself, splits. It is the continuous alternation of rest and movement that creates life: a game of causes and effects, behind which there is something perpetually motionless. Wisdom is coming to perceive this point of absolute stillness present in us: the eye of the cyclone.

9. IMPOTENCE

You are overwhelmed by events: you cannot do anything to help the situation evolve, nor can you cause any change. Accept this impotence. This, too, is love.

10. YOUR INNER GUIDE

The Oracle reminds you that within you there is a guide able to root you in happiness, yet you do not use it, so that you are not aware of it. Don't worry: it can be revitalized, indeed it must be awakened... if you want to live love to the fullest.

11. HARMONY: LOVE AND PEACE

In this fusion of love we find ourselves immersed in the fullness of the present: in it is complete fulfillment. Allow yourself to be lost in the brevity of this instant, in the arms of your loved one. Do not ask for anything else!

12. SUPERFICIALITY

Let's not delude ourselves: one loves for a variety of reasons and all lead to stagnation. The *I Ching* advises you to withdraw into yourself, into your secret intimacy, to give depth to love.

13. TO BE IN LOVE

Every love has within it a message of openness, which is not to impose one's own will, but to transmit the meaning and vibration of being in tune with the universal force that governs the whole of existence. Love is power in itself and for itself, it does not impose itself: it limits itself to sharing.

14. TOTALITY

Times are good: you have a mastery of life that allows you total freedom of action. And the fact that it is not selfishness is demonstrated by your not doing anything to make this harmony happen.

15. UNIQUENESS

Love happens and is not anything flashy: it reveals itself in an image of modesty that the hexagram illustrates as "the mountain, below" that hides "in the earth, above". The Oracle is a favorable omen.

16. FERVOR

The Oracle bears witness to the happy impetus of the force that, once shared, becomes fervor. Success is due to abandoning oneself to the power of love: the absence of resistance is the only thing required.

17. LOOKING AT ONE ANOTHER
The Oracle speaks of something that unfolds "looking at one another". The meaning is simple: acceptance of the state of things. In this harmonization, which is not condescension, nor requires compromise, one enters into the natural rhythm of the world.

18. AWARENESS
The hexagram shows a static situation. The Oracle does not want to judge this state of affairs, but invites us to reflect on the mechanisms or conditioning that generate it, and on the inner qualities to be focused on to get out of a situation of stagnation in which you will only rot.

19. LISTENING TO ONE ANOTHER
The Oracle heralds prosperity. You are evolving within a situation that, day after day, matures and bears fruit.

20. CONTEMPLATION
Within the Taoist doctrine, this hexagram as a whole represents the worldview of the wise man: *Kuan* is objectless attention, not limited by the ego. In practice, it is meditation... the other side of love: learn to include it in your game of life.

21. BETRAYING (JEALOUSY)

Are you experiencing the dark side of love? Take the time to assimilate betrayal. In those desperate moments what we loved in the other appears with absolute certainty: observe it and do it yourself, keeping your awareness. In this attentive presence, grow, evolve: become yourself.

22. TOUCHING ONE ANOTHER

Apparently the Oracle is in favor. For a moment you find yourself living in a dimension free from any apprehension... you flow in spite of yourself. However, the Oracle also warns: since all this is caused by something external to you, it inevitably depends on that catalyst. So it is unstable.

23. THE WEAR AND TEAR OF TIME

Despite love opening up to something eternal, since it is born in time it is destined to perish, despite the best intentions. The Oracle indicates the attitude to adopt: remain firm as a mountain, keep an absolute stillness, and let yourself be crossed by what happens to you... this will also pass.

24. A NEW BEGINNING

You're in front of a new beginning. Try asking yourself, "Where is the real light source that I call love?" In this way, thanks to the impulse of love, you will approach your inner center. And you will see your original nature: that intimate and deep flame that dwells in the depths of your being.

25. THE INNOCENCE OF THE CHILD
The hexagram evokes the natural state of things. It is an invitation to act naturally, just as a child does: this is true irreproachable behaviour.

26. FEAR OF LOVE
The Oracle indicates that you are enjoying considerable strength, so it's the right time to progress... draw from the current state of power the courage to dare a total abandonment... don't retreat! Many do not dare in love, contenting themselves with lukewarm compromises, out of fear.

27. NOURISHMENT
This is the right measure of love: a precious nourishment, more than food, which the Oracle advises not to miss if you wish to maintain a healthy psychophysical balance.

28. UNDER PRESSURE
The situation is very serious: the difficulties seem to be insurmountable. The position you are in is desperate, to

say the least. How to get out of it? Keep a joyful serenity. No matter how serious the danger is... rooted in trust, this is the time to focus on your beating heart.

29. THE DARK NIGHT OF THE SOUL
You are experiencing the confrontation with the existential anguish that, suddenly, can darken life. The Oracle traces the simple way out: you have to get to the heart of things and not stop at the surface of events. In this sense, the prophesy is positive: whatever the darkness in which you are immersed, in you there is the awareness that can grasp the teaching. Anchor yourself to that!

30. FALLING IN LOVE
The hexagram embodies "nature in its splendor", therefore the Oracle is simple: what you are living through raises your heart and spirit, and puts you in touch with the everlasting and imperishable splendor that is love. Let this flame burn completely, without expecting anything else.

31. ENGAGEMENT
The Oracle speaks of the union of essential forces, so the prophecy is a happy one. Be receptive to this state of affairs; simply let what is happening, by its very nature, happen!

32. LONG TERM COMMITMENT

The Oracle invites you to expressly avoid routine. Immersed in daily life, love dies at the outset. Its endurance comes from never-ending transformation, and therefore of continuous renewal.

33. DECEPTION

Something is causing love to run away... In fact, that energy is retreating, folding back on itself to protect itself: it cannot do otherwise. In short, you will be exhausted... and you won't see even the shadow of love anymore!

34. TRUST

The hexagram indicates the power of strength, firmness. The Oracle is therefore saying that you have the opportunity to achieve true greatness: you only have to evolve according to the nature of things.

35. GAME OF LOVE

The prophecy is favourable: it speaks of expansion. You have finally understood that love is a game... nothing in you prevents it from being what it is anymore.

36. OBSESSION AND GREED

The light of love is dimmed by primordial or mental forces that have the upper hand. Its naturalness is suffocated or obscured by something that prevents its free expression as a simple need. Try to intervene on those conditions that have clouded your imagination and your ability to live fluidly.

37. FAMILY
This hexagram speaks of the family: it is the voice of a son who complains about the fate of his mother, once a tender branch, now a thorny fagot from the effort of raising ungrateful children. The Oracle invites you to see the meaning of your deep love, within the family.

38. "NO" IN LOVE
This is about unrequited love. The Oracle speaks of immense diversity, disunity, separation. The two wills at stake each express themselves by themselves and do not meet, they do not harmonize.

39. THE OBSTACLE
A terrifying abyss is accompanied by an insurmountable peak. There seems to be no way out: the danger is accompanied by paralysis. A means must be found to indirectly overcome these obstacles. What to do? It is time for meditation and awareness.

40. LIBERATION

The Oracle indicates a true, real liberation, different from our way of interpreting the term 'liberation': it is neither the denial of desire, nor its attainment.

41. SUFFERING

Step by step, every joy condenses, stiffens, freezes. The joyful impulse decreases... it is a natural law. This too is living! We would like to grasp only joy, but it is the sublime ecstasy of love that unleashes the most terrible agony.

42. LOVE YOURSELF

The Oracle is an invitation: love yourself. In fact, the real problem is that you often don't even accept yourself! How many times have you done what you really liked? Start now, here, immediately...

43. THE COURAGE OF LOVE

The Oracle itself is indefinite: it's a simple warning. If you tense up in rejection, the power of love will not be able to do anything. Conversely, if that strength takes on a sense of courage within you - both to love and to accept love - then...

44. INTIMATE MEETING
The Oracle is a warning: if such an intimate and profound encounter is linked to simple seduction - of a man or a woman - catastrophe is certain to follow.

45. HAPPINESS IS TO LOVE
Beyond the simple reality of the couple, the Oracle speaks of success, as soon as the aspect of love is extended as an instrument of bonding with the human union. To do so is simple: to love is sufficient.

46. SEX
At the beginning of a union, love is sexuality. To evolve, it is necessary to abandon oneself to the simplest game of love, this is the invitation of the Oracle.

47. FAILURE
Every passion runs out of energy... but the interpretation is delicate; it should not be read in a negative way: what is happening is part of the circle of life. Do you feel empty, or emptied? It is not a *bad thing*, on the contrary... now it's time to come back to yourself: the season of solitude is approaching. Learn to dance between encounters and separations.

48. THE SPRING

The image depicts what is deepest in us humans: it evokes our essential nature. The Oracle is simple: do not lose contact with that intimate inner reality, because it is from there that you extract - consciously or not - the life force that animates all your gestures, your whole life.

49. THE TOMB OF LOVE

In marriage there is a repression, a domestication of love in function of other interests, of the ego's primordial fears, which mark its end. The Oracle signals that it is time for revolution: evaluate what your life is based on. The invitation is to regenerate yourself: in you there is always a creative force capable of renewing and renewing yourself eternally.

50. THE CRUCIBLE

The Oracle is an invitation to root your love in the aspect of honesty and sincerity; you can do it, using your energy not to depend on your partner for your survival... at all levels!

51. FATAL EVENT

The Oracle's advice is to live this moment of intensity for what it is: it will leave an intimate and everlasting trace in your life. Enter deeply into the present moment: feel yourself quivering, listen to that quiver... let the heart speak to the heart. It happens... we only need to eliminate every obstacle to its happening. It is only in this way that love continues to recreate itself.

52. WITNESS

If you are in a state of upheaval, if love is upsetting you with its upheaval... find in yourself a space of calmness in which to hang out!

53. INTIMACY

The dimension in which the Oracle speaks is not the sphere of security, possession and jealousy. Intimacy, which is the invisible mountain of love, has its roots in something that cannot be grasped by any of the five senses. It is nothing but emptiness and silence.

54. THE YOUNG BRIDE

All free relations between human beings are represented here. For the *I Ching* the strength of love is such that it breaks and eliminates every convention and every rule established by social norms. The Oracle speaks of the superior harmony that love brings about in the world.

55. FULLNESS

For the Oracle this is a moment of fullness... the blazing fire of the life force erupts with the roar of thunder, annulling and cancelling all inhibition of consciousness. Any sense of apathy has vanished: you are faced with a vital experience. Perhaps you perceive it as death, don't be afraid: for the first time... you are living!

56. THE WAYFARER
The omen speaks to the traveler within you. As you move from one experience to another, meeting friends and lovers, you are a traveler. Something prevents you from stopping forever: you try and try again, and every time you feel like you have reached a permanent home. But there comes a moment, and that's it, when you feel like you have to resume the journey...

57. WIND
The Oracle invites you to look at existence: everything that happens to you, everything, directly... as simple naked and raw facts, without putting labels, without saying right or wrong, good or bad. It leaves aside the mind and its eternal judgment.

58. FRIENDSHIP
It is a fluid communication between two beings that permeate each other... without penetrating each other! The Oracle suggests that, in spite of yourselves, thanks to your intimacy, your relationship with your partner has transformed itself into friendship.

59. ALONENESS

The Oracle invites you to fully immerse yourself in your being. This card marks the end of the many experiences in the outer world and indicates the way forward to further evolve. At the peak of so many experiences, with the dissolution of selfishness - the idea of being a separate small self fighting against everything and everyone - we find ourselves alone. In the intimate union that is the essence of life, you are alone!

60. LIMITATION

The hexagram warns: by imposing too strict limits on love, you prevent its freedom and free flow; you hinder its never/ending evolution.

61. THE PRESENT MOMENT

The hexagram offers the image of a free heart, able to perceive the truth and to welcome it within itself. The Oracle is an invitation to immerse oneself in one's own present truth, to live in the real "here and now"-time in which the whole of existence dwells.

62. IDENTIFICATIONS

The Oracle warns: be careful of the identifications! Of course, love opens to an unparalleled fullness and bliss, but if you identify that fullness with a person, you open yourself to immense spaces of pain and misfortune, forcing oneself and the other to a very heavy slavery or dependence.

63. TRANSFIGURATION

Everything comes to wholeness, to complete resolution, transfigures and makes contact with the dimension of the spirit... it is but a moment, which hides within itself the signs of decline. Immerse yourself as much as you can in this dimension, before it becomes a memory, an illusion, a dream...

64. THE MYSTICAL UNION

The Oracle speaks of a missed encounter... one yearns for something, one hopes, but the resolution does not come. It is a warning: in the intimate communion that love with a lover engenders, one comes to grasp the possible fusion that is completion and realization. It is a flash of precious intuition, but elusive... that is why it is fundamental to link love to meditation.

I CHING DELL'AMORE

METODO DI LETTURA SEMPLIFICATO

Trova un momento per stare con te stesso, in un ambiente appartato, libero dalle comuni sollecitazioni. Rilassati semplicemente osservando il respiro e, quando senti di poter stabilire un contatto con il tuo sé più intimo, mischia le carte: i 64 esagrammi tradizionali del *Libro dei Mutamenti* sono stati letti in funzione dell'amore e tradotti in immagini che ne rendono più immediato l'impatto. Visualizza interiormente la tua attuale esperienza dell'amore: lasciala affiorare di fronte a te per ciò che è, non giudicarla, non interpretarla, non volerla diversa; e non è necessario verbalizzare alcuna domanda. Ricorda: non stai cercando consolazioni, né vuoi modificare ciò che ti accade: vuoi comprendere. Quando ti senti pronto, distendi il mazzo e, con la mano sinistra, gira una carta: leggi la descrizione e contempla l'immagine, osservando come fa luce sul tuo stato di cose. Chiudi gli occhi e medita in silenzio il messaggio. L'accettazione è la prima chiave di lettura, perché è in grado di produrre un cambiamento, ma soprattutto è capace di aiutarti a vedere in modo distaccato l'esperienza che la vita ti sta offrendo… e ricorda: anche questo passerà, è soltanto una stagione della tua vita. Pertanto accogli in te quanto la carta ti suggerisce, senza abbatterti o esaltarti. È questa la lezione fondamentale dell'*I Ching dell'Amore*.

LE SENTENZE

1. IL DESIDERIO CREATIVO

La tradizione orientale vede nel desiderio l'inizio dell'universo. Questa carta è un invito a non complicarsi la vita: *accetta il desiderio.* Non è bene lottare contro la sessualità. Ogni repressione ti metterà in lotta contro te stesso… e per giungere alla piena realizzazione hai bisogno di tutte le tue forze. La carta segnala che sei in sintonia con la potenza creativa dell'universo.

2. LA RICETTIVITÀ

Questa carta è un segno di forte presenza *Yin*, cioè di ricettività, nella tua vita. Osserva come ti governa, cosa implica e cosa ne deriva: in te la forza creativa sta sedimentando e acquistando concretezza.

3. LA DIFFICOLTÀ INIZIALE

L'Oracolo offre un invito a non ridurre l'altro a un oggetto d'uso, né a vendersi in nome dell'amore, bensì ad abbandonarsi al magnetismo cosmico che nell'amore si attiva.

4. L'INESPERIENZA GIOVANILE

L'Oracolo ti sta indicando che sei di fronte a un abisso, ma non ti preoccupare: per necessità la spensieratezza che caratterizza questa carta ti porta a fluire, superando così qualsiasi ostacolo ti impedisca di progredire.

5. L'ATTESA

In amore è importante lasciare che l'amore in sé si compia. L'attesa è un incantesimo… Per un attimo si viene in contatto con la propria essenza e in essa ci si raccoglie. L'Oracolo dice che sei in attesa. Non volere altro!

6. IL CONFLITTO

Di solito coloriamo l'amore di sogni e fantasie, di pretese e credenze, impedendogli di esistere o condizionandolo fino a deformarlo. È il tuo caso? Osserva come hai manipolato il tuo amore.

7. LA COESIONE

In ogni realtà della vita, e soprattutto in amore, è bene avere in sé un fulcro di coesione, così qualsiasi incontro sarà una condivisione e potrai arricchirti ed espanderti al contatto con l'altro. Ricentrati in te stesso!

8. SOLIDARIETÀ DEI COMPLEMENTARI

Il Tao, per manifestarsi, si sdoppia. È il continuo alternarsi di riposo e movimento che crea la vita: un gioco di cause ed effetti, dietro al quale esiste qualcosa di perennemente immobile. Saggezza è giungere a percepire questo punto di assoluta quiete presente in noi: l'occhio del ciclone.

9. L'IMPOTENZA

Sei travolto dagli avvenimenti: non puoi far nulla per far evolvere la situazione, né puoi provocare alcun cambiamento. Accetta questa impotenza. Anche questo è amore.

10. LA TUA GUIDA INTERIORE

L'Oracolo ti ricorda che dentro di te hai una guida in grado di radicarti nella felicità, eppure non la usi; addirittura non ne sei consapevole! Non preoccuparti: può essere rivitalizzata, anzi, va risvegliata, se vuoi vivere in pienezza l'amore.

11. L'ARMONIA: AMORE E PACE

In ogni fusione d'amore ci si trova immersi nella pienezza del presente: in esso è totale appagamento. Concediti di perderti nella brevità di questo istante, tra le braccia della persona amata. Non chiedere altro!

12. LA SUPERFICIALITÀ

Non illudiamoci: facilmente, si ama per le ragioni più diverse e tutte portano al ristagno. L'*I Ching* consiglia di ritirarti in te stesso, nella tua segreta intimità, per dare profondità all'amore.

13. ESSERE IN AMORE

Qualsiasi amore ha in sé un messaggio di apertura, che non è imporre il proprio volere, bensì trasmettere il senso e la vibrazione dell'essere in sintonia con la forza universale che governa l'esistenza intera. L'amore è potenza in sé e per sé, non si impone: si limita a condividere.

14. LA TOTALITÀ

I tempi sono favorevoli: hai una padronanza sulla vita che ti permette totale libertà d'azione. E il fatto che non si tratti d'egoismo è dimostrato dal tuo non fare nulla perché questa armonia accada.

15. UNICITÀ

L'amore accade e non è nulla di appariscente: si rivela in un'immagine di modestia che l'esagramma illustra come "la montagna, in basso" che si nasconde "nella terra, in alto". L'Oracolo è un presagio favorevole.

16. IL FERVORE

L'Oracolo testimonia l'impeto felice della forza che, una volta condivisa, diventa fervore. Il successo è dato dall'abbandonarsi alla forza dell'amore: l'assenza di resistenza è la sola cosa richiesta.

17. GUARDARSI

L'Oracolo parla di qualcosa che accade "guardandosi". Il significato è semplice: accettazione dello stato di cose. In questo armonizzarsi, che non è condiscendenza né richiede compromessi, si partecipa al ritmo naturale del mondo.

18. PRENDERE COSCIENZA

L'esagramma raffigura una situazione statica. L'Oracolo non vuole giudicare questo stato di cose, ma invita a riflettere su meccanismi o condizionamenti che lo generano, e sulle qualità interiori da mettere a fuoco per uscire da una situazione di ristagno in cui si può solo marcire.

19. ASCOLIARSI

L'Oracolo dà un presagio di prosperità. Stai evolvendo all'interno di una situazione che, giorno dopo giorno, matura e fruttifica.

20. LA CONTEMPLAZIONE

Nel suo insieme, all'interno della dottrina taoista, questo esagramma rappresenta la visione del mondo del saggio: *Kuan* è attenzione priva di oggetto, non limitata dall'ego. In pratica è meditazione… l'altra faccia dell'amore: impara a includerla nel tuo quotidiano.

21. TRADIRSI (LA GELOSIA)

Stai vivendo il lato oscuro dell'amore? Concediti il tempo necessario per assimilare il tradimento. In quegli attimi disperanti appare con assoluta certezza ciò che nell'altro amavamo: osservalo e fallo tuo, mantenendone in te la coscienza. In questa presenza attenta, cresci ed evolvi: diventi te stesso o te stessa.

22. TOCCARSI

In apparenza l'Oracolo è favorevole. Per un attimo ci si trova a vivere in una dimensione libera da qualsiasi inquietudine… si fluisce nostro malgrado. Tuttavia l'Oracolo mette anche in guardia: poiché tutto questo è provocato da qualcosa di esterno a te, inevitabilmente dipende da quell'elemento catalizzatore, dunque è instabile.

23. L'USURA DEL TEMPO

Malgrado l'amore schiuda a qualcosa di eterno, poiché nasce nel tempo è destinato a perire, nonostante le migliori intenzioni. L'Oracolo indica l'atteggiamento da adottare: resta saldo come una montagna, conserva un'immobilità assoluta, e lasciati attraversare da ciò che ti accade - anche questo passerà.

24. UN NUOVO INIZIO

Sei di fronte a un nuovo inizio. Prova a chiederti: "Dov'è la vera sorgente luminosa che chiamo amore?" In questo modo, grazie all'impulso dell'amore, ti avvicinerai al tuo centro interiore, e vedrai il tuo volto originale: quella fiamma intima e profonda che dimora negli abissi del tuo essere.

25. L'INNOCENZA DEL BAMBINO

L'esagramma evoca lo stato naturale delle cose. È un invito ad agire con naturalezza, proprio come fa un bambino: questo è il vero comportamento irreprensibile.

26. LA PAURA DELL'AMORE

L'Oracolo indica che stai godendo di una forza notevole, dunque è il momento giusto per progredire. Trai dallo stato attuale di potenza il coraggio per abbandonarti totalmente… non ritrarti! Per paura, molti non osano in amore, accontentandosi di tiepidi compromessi.

27. IL NUTRIMENTO

Questa è la giusta misura dell'amore: un nutrimento prezioso, più del cibo, che l'Oracolo consiglia di non farsi mancare, se si vuole conservare un sano equilibrio psicofisico.

28. SOTTO PRESSIONE

La situazione è gravissima: le difficoltà sembrano insuperabili. La posizione in cui ti trovi è a dir poco disperata. Come uscirne? Conserva una serenità gioiosa. Non importa quanto il pericolo sia grave... radicati nella fiducia, questo è il momento per mettere a fuoco il tuo cuore pulsante.

29. LA BUIA NOTTE DELL'ANIMA

Stai vivendo l'impatto con l'angoscia esistenziale che, a sorpresa, può oscurare la vita. L'Oracolo traccia la semplice via d'uscita: occorre andare al cuore delle cose e non fermarsi alla superficie degli eventi. In questo senso, il presagio è positivo: qualsiasi sia l'oscurità in cui sei immerso, in te esiste la consapevolezza in grado di coglierne l'insegnamento. Ancorati a quella!

30. L'INNAMORAMENTO

L'esagramma incarna "la natura nel suo splendore", pertanto l'Oracolo è semplice: ciò che stai vivendo innalza il cuore e lo spirito, e ti mette in contatto con lo splendore perenne e imperituro dell'amore. Lascia ardere totalmente questa fiamma, senza pretendere altro.

31. IL FIDANZAMENTO

L'Oracolo parla di unione di forze essenziali, il presagio è dunque felice. Sii ricettivo a ciò che accade: abbandonati a ciò che, semplicemente, sta accadendo!

32. LA DURATA

L'Oracolo invita a evitare espressamente la routine. Immerso nella vita quotidiana, l'amore muore d'acchito. La durata è data da una perenne trasformazione, e dunque da un continuo rinnovamento.

33. L'INGANNO

Qualcosa sta mettendo in fuga l'amore. Di fatto quell'energia si sta ritirando, ripiega in se stessa per proteggersi: non può fare altrimenti. In breve tu sarai esausto, e dell'amore non vedrai più nemmeno l'ombra!

34. FIDUCIA

L'esagramma indica il potere della forza, la fermezza. L'Oracolo dunque sta dicendo che hai l'opportunità di conseguire la vera grandezza: occorre solo evolversi naturalmente.

35. IL GIOCO DELL'AMORE

Il presagio è favorevole: parla di espansione. Finalmente hai compreso che l'amore è un gioco... nulla in te gli impedisce più di accadere.

36. OSSESSIONE (AVIDITÀ)

La luce dell'amore è oscurata da forze primordiali o mentali che hanno preso il sopravvento. La sua naturalezza è soffocata o oscurata da qualcosa che ne impedisce la libera espressione di semplice bisogno dell'anima. Vedi di intervenire sui condizionamenti che hanno offuscato la tua immaginazione, la tua capacità di vivere fluidamente.

37. LA FAMIGLIA

Questo esagramma parla della famiglia: è la voce di un figlio che lamenta la sorte della madre, un giorno tenero ramo, ora fatta fascina spinosa per la fatica di allevare figli ingrati. L'Oracolo invita a vedere il senso del proprio amore profondo, in seno alla famiglia.

38. IL NO IN AMORE

Si tratta di amore non corrisposto. L'Oracolo parla di diversità incolmabili, disunione, separazione. Le due volontà in gioco si esprimono ciascuna per sé e non s'incontrano, non si armonizzano.

39. L'OSTACOLO

Un abisso terrificante si accompagna a una vetta insormontabile. Pare non esserci via d'uscita: il pericolo si accompagna alla paralisi. Occorre trovare un mezzo per vincere indirettamente questi ostacoli. Che fare? È tempo di meditazione e consapevolezza.

40. LA LIBERAZIONE

L'Oracolo indica una liberazione vera, reale, diversa dal nostro interpretare il termine 'liberazione': non è la negazione del desiderio, né il suo conseguimento. È osservazione distaccata e neutrale.

41. LA SOFFERENZA

Passo dopo passo, ogni piacere si condensa, si irrigidisce, si pietrifica. L'impulso gioioso si riduce, è una legge naturale. Anche questo è vivere! Noi vorremmo cogliere solo la gioia, ma è l'estasi sublime dell'amore a scatenare l'agonia più atroce.

42. AMA TE STESSO

L'Oracolo è un preciso invito: ama te stesso. Di fatto, il vero problema è che spesso non ti accetti neppure! Quante volte hai fatto ciò che ti dava vero piacere? Inizia ora, qui, subito!

43. IL CORAGGIO DELL'AMORE

L'Oracolo in sé è indefinito: è un semplice avvertimento. Se ti irrigidisci nel rifiuto, la forza dell'amore verrà ostacolata. Viceversa, se quella forza assume in te il senso del coraggio – sia di amare, sia di accettare l'amore allora…

44. L'INCONTRO INTIMO

L'Oracolo è un monito: se un incontro così intimo e profondo è legato a semplice seduzione – dell'uomo o della donna – ne conseguirà sicura catastrofe.

45. FELICITÀ È AMARE

Al di là della semplice realtà di coppia, l'Oracolo parla di buona riuscita, allorché si estende la dimensione dell'amore a strumento di coesione con il consorzio umano. Farlo è semplice: amare è sufficiente.

46. IL SESSO

All'inizio dell'unione, l'amore è sessualità. Per evolvere, occorre abbandonarsi al gioco più semplice dell'amore: questo è l'invito dell'Oracolo.

47. IL FALLIMENTO

Ogni passione si esaurisce… ma l'interpretazione è delicata; non va letta in maniera negativa: ciò che sta accadendo è parte del ciclo della vita. Ti senti vuoto, svuotato? Non è *un male*, anzi, ora è tempo di tornare a sé stessi: si avvicina la stagione della solitudine. Impara a danzare tra incontri e separazioni.

48. LA SORGENTE

L'immagine raffigura ciò che vi è di più profondo in noi umani: evoca la nostra natura essenziale. L'Oracolo è semplice: non perdere contatto con quell'intima interiorità, perché è da lì che affiora – cosciente o meno – la forza vitale che anima ogni tuo gesto, l'intera tua vita.

49. LA TOMBA DELL'AMORE

Nel matrimonio esiste una repressione, un addomesticamento dell'amore in funzione di altri interessi, di paure primarie dell'io, che ne siglano la fine. L'Oracolo segnala che è tempo di rivoluzione: valuta su cosa si fonda la tua vita. L'invito è a rigenerarti: in te esiste una forza creatrice in grado di rinnovare e di rinnovarti perennemente.

50. IL CROGIUOLO

L'Oracolo è un invito a radicare il tuo amore nella dimensione dell'onestà e della sincerità: puoi farlo, usando la tua energia per non dipendere dal partner per la tua sopravvivenza… a tutti i livelli!

51 L'EVENTO FATALE

Il consiglio dell'Oracolo è vivere questo attimo di intensità per ciò che è: lascerà una traccia intima e perenne nella tua vita. Entra in profondità nell'istante presente: sentiti fremere, ascolta quel brivido, lascia che il cuore parli al cuore. Accade… occorre solo eliminare ogni ostacolo al suo accadere. Solo così l'amore continua a ricrearsi.

52. IL TESTIMONE

Se sei in uno stato di turbamento, se l'amore ti sta sconvolgendo con il suo turbinare… crea in te uno spazio di quiete in cui sostare!

53. L'INTIMITÀ

La dimensione in cui l'Oracolo parla non è la sfera delle sicurezze, del possesso e della gelosia. L'intimità, che è l'invisibile montagna dell'amore, ha fondamenta in qualcosa che non può essere afferrato da nessuno dei cinque sensi. Non è che vuoto e silenzio.

54. LA GIOVANE SPOSA

Sono qui raffigurate tutte le libere relazioni tra esseri umani. Per l'*I Ching* la forza dell'amore è tale da spezzare ed eliminare ogni convenzione e ogni regola fissata dalle norme sociali. L'Oracolo parla dell'armonia superiore che l'amore induce nel mondo.

55. LA PIENEZZA

Per l'Oracolo questo è un attimo di pienezza: il fuoco ardente della forza vitale erompe con fragore di tuono, annullandosi e annullando ogni inibizione della coscienza. Qualsiasi senso di apatia è svanito: sei di fronte a un'esperienza vitale. Forse la percepisci come una morte dell'io, ma non devi temere: per la prima volta... stai vivendo!

56. IL VIANDANTE

Il presagio parla al viandante che c'è in te. Nel tuo passare da un'esperienza all'altra, nell'incontrare amici e amanti, sei un viandante. Qualcosa ti impedisce di fermarti per sempre: ci provi e ci riprovi, e ogni volta ti sembra di aver raggiunto una dimora stabile. Ma viene un momento, ed è questo, in cui senti di dover riprendere il cammino.

57. IL VENTO

L'Oracolo invita a guardare l'esistenza: tutto ciò che ti accade, ogni cosa, osservalo *direttamente*… come semplici fatti nudi e crudi, senza porre etichette, senza dire giusto o sbagliato, buono o cattivo. Lascia in disparte la mente e il suo perenne giudizio.

58. L'AMICIZIA

È una comunicazione fluida tra due esseri che si compenetrano… senza penetrarsi! L'Oracolo indica che, vostro malgrado, grazie all'intimità, la relazione che hai con il tuo partner si è mutata in amicizia.

59. LA SOLITUDINE

L'Oracolo invita a immergersi pienamente nel proprio essere. Questa carta segna il termine delle tantissime esperienze nel mondo esteriore e indica la via da seguire per compiere un'ulteriore evoluzione. Al culmine di tante esperienze, dissolto l'egoismo – l'idea di essere un piccolo io separato e in lotta contro tutto e tutti – ci si ritrova soli. Nell'intima unione che è l'essenza della vita, si è soli!

60. LA LIMITAZIONE

L'esagramma avverte: imponendo limiti troppo severi all'amore ne impedisci la libertà e il libero fluire, ne ostacoli la perenne evoluzione.

61. IL MOMENTO PRESENTE

L'esagramma offre l'immagine di un cuore libero, in grado di percepire il Vero e di accoglierlo dentro di sé. L'Oracolo è un invito a immergersi nella propria verità presente: vivi *"quieora"* – nel tempo reale in cui l'intera esistenza dimora!

62. LE IDENTIFICAZIONI

L'Oracolo ammonisce: stai attento alle identificazioni! Certo, l'amore dona una pienezza e a una beatitudine senza confronti, ma se si identifica quella pienezza con una persona, ci si apre a spazi di dolore e di sciagura immensi, costringendo sé stessi e l'altro a una pesantissima schiavitù o dipendenza.

63. LA TRASFIGURAZIONE

Ogni cosa giunge a pienezza, a completa risoluzione, trasfigura e mette in contatto con la dimensione dello spirito… è un attimo, che nasconde in sé i segni della decadenza. Immergiti e vivi quanto più puoi in questa dimensione, prima che diventi un ricordo, un'illusione, un sogno.

64. L'UNIONE MISTICA

L'Oracolo parla di un mancato incontro; si anela a qualcosa, si spera, ma la fusione non accade. È un monito: nell'intima comunione generata dall'amore con un amante, si giunge a cogliere la possibile *Unione mistica* che è completamento e realizzazione. È un lampo d'intuizione prezioso, ma ineffabile - per questo è fondamentale unire l'amore alla meditazione.

I CHING
DEL AMOR

MÉTODO DE LECTURA SIMPLIFICADO

Busca un momento para estar contigo mismo, en un ambiente apartado, libre de las interrupciones habituales. Relájate simplemente observando la respiración y, cuando sientas que puedes establecer un contacto con tú yo más íntimo, baraja las cartas: los 64 hexagramas tradicionales del *I Ching* (Libro de las Mutaciones) se han leído en materia amorosa y se han traducido en imágenes de impacto inmediato. Visualiza interiormente tu actual experiencia del amor: déjala aflorar ante ti tal como es, sin juzgarla, sin interpretarla, sin querer cambiarla; no es necesario verbalizar ninguna pregunta. Recuerda: no estas buscando consuelos, ni quieres modificar lo que te sucede: quieres entender. Cuando estés listo, extiende la baraja y, con la mano izquierda, gira una carta: lee la descripción y contempla la imagen, observando cómo arroja luz cerca de tu situación. Cierra los ojos y medita en silencio el mensaje. La aceptación es la primera clave de lectura, porque es capaz de producir un cambio, pero sobre todo es capaz de ayudarte a ver con distancia la experiencia que la vida te está ofreciendo... y recuerda: esto también pasará, solo es una fase de tu vida. Por lo tanto interioriza lo que la carta te sugiere, sin desanimarte ni exaltarte. Esta es la lección fundamental del *I Ching del Amor*.

LAS SENTENCIAS

1. EL DESEO CREATIVO

Según la tradición oriental el deseo es el inicio del universo. Esta carta es una invitación a no complicarse la vida: *acepta el deseo*. No conviene luchar contra la sexualidad. Cualquier represión te provocará una lucha interior... y para alcanzar la realización plena necesitas todas tus fuerzas. La carta indica que estás en sintonía con la potencia creativa del universo.

2. LA RECEPTIVIDAD

Esta carta es un indicio de fuerte presencia *Yin*, es decir de receptividad, en tu vida. Observa cómo rige tu vida, qué implica y cuáles son sus consecuencias: la fuerza creativa se está asentando en ti y se está materializando.

3. LA DIFICULTAD INICIAL

El Oráculo invita a no reducir al prójimo a un objeto de uso, ni a venderse en nombre del amor, sino a abandonarse al magnetismo cósmico que se activa en el amor.

4. LA EXPERIENCIA JUVENIL

El Oráculo te está indicando que estás ante un abismo, pero no te preocupes: por necesidad la despreocupación que caracteriza esta carta te hace fluir, superando así cualquier obstáculo que te impida progresar.

5. LA ESPERA

En el amor, es importante dejar que este se manifieste. La espera es un hechizo... Por un momento entramos en contacto con la propia esencia y nos fundimos con esta. El Oráculo dice que estás a la espera. ¡No desees nada más!

6. EL CONFLICTO

Generalmente pintamos el amor de sueños y fantasías, de expectativas e ilusiones, impidiéndole existir o condicionándolo hasta deformarlo. ¿Es tu caso? Observa cómo has manipulado tu amor.

7. LA COHESIÓN

En cualquier realidad de la vida, y sobre todo en el amor, conviene tener un punto de cohesión, así cualquier encuentro será un momento compartido y podrás enriquecerte y expandirte gracias al contacto con el otro. ¡Céntrate en ti mismo!

8. SOLIDARIDAD CON LOS COMPLEMENTARIOS

El Tao, para manifestarse, se desdobla. La alternancia continua de reposo y movimiento crea la vida: un juego de causas y efectos, tras el cual existe algo perennemente inmóvil. La sabiduría es alcanzar este punto de absoluta paz presente en nosotros: el ojo del ciclón.

9. LA IMPOTENCIA

Te superan los acontecimientos: no puedes hacer nada para que la situación evolucione, ni puedes provocar cambio alguno. Acepta esta impotencia. También esto es amor.

10. TU GUÍA INTERIOR

El Oráculo te recuerda que dentro de ti hay un guía capaz de conducirte a la felicidad, pero no lo usas; ¡ni siquiera eres consciente de que lo tienes! No te preocupes: puedes revitalizarlo, es más, debes despertarlo, si quieres vivir el amor plenamente.

11. LA ARMONÍA: AMOR Y PAZ

En toda fusión amorosa nos encontramos inmersos en la plenitud del presente: en este la satisfacción es total. Permítete la licencia de perderte en la brevedad de este instante, entre los brazos de la persona amada. ¡No pidas nada más!

12. LA SUPERFICIALIDAD

No te hagas ilusiones: fácilmente, se ama por los motivos más variados y todos conducen al estancamiento. El *I Ching* te aconseja recogerte en ti mismo, en tu secreta intimidad, para dar profundidad al amor.

13. ESTADO DE AMOR

Cualquier amor encierra en sí mismo un mensaje de apertura, que no consiste en imponer el propio deseo, sino en transmitir el sentido y la vibración del ser en sintonía con la fuerza universal que rige toda la existencia. El amor es potencia en sí y de por sí, no se impone: nos limitamos a compartirlo.

14. LA TOTALIDAD

Los tiempos son favorables: tienes un dominio de tu vida que te permite actuar con total libertad. Y no se trata de egoísmo, puesto que tú no haces nada para que esta armonía se manifieste.

15. UNICIDAD

El amor sucede y no es nada ostentoso: se revela en una imagen de modestia que el hexagrama ilustra como «la montaña, abajo» que se oculta «en la tierra, arriba». El Oráculo es un presagio favorable.

16. EL FERVOR

El Oráculo demuestra el ímpetu feliz de la fuerza que, una vez compartida, se convierte en fervor. El éxito consiste en abandonarse a la fuerza del amor: solo se pide no oponer resistencia.

17. OBSERVARSE

El Oráculo habla de algo que sucede «al mirarse». El significado es sencillo: aceptar las cosas como son. En esta armonía, que no es condescendencia ni pedir renuncias, se participa al ritmo natural del mundo.

18. TOMAR CONCIENCIA

El hexagrama representa una situación estática. El Oráculo no quiere juzgar esta situación, sino que invita a reflexionar sobre los mecanismos o los condicionamientos que la provocan, y sobre las cualidades interiores que deben cultivarse para salir de una situación de estancamiento en la que solo se puede zozobrar.

19. ESCUCHARSE

El Oráculo hace un presagio de prosperidad. Estás evolucionando en una situación que, día tras día, madura y fructifica.

20. LA CONTEMPLACIÓN

En su conjunto, en la doctrina taoísta, este hexagrama representa la visión del mundo del sabio: *Kuan* es atención sin objeto, no limitada por el ego. En la práctica es meditación... la otra cara del amor: aprende a incluirla en tu día a día.

21. TRAICIONARSE (LOS CELOS)

¿Estás viviendo el lado oscuro del amor? Tómate el tiempo necesario para asimilar la traición. En esos momentos desesperantes aparece con certeza absoluta lo que amábamos en el otro: obsérvalo y hazlo tuyo, manteniendo la conciencia en ti. En esta presencia atenta, crece y evoluciona: sé tú mismo o tú misma.

22. TOCARSE

Parece que el Oráculo es favorable. Por un momento se vive en una dimensión libre de cualquier preocupación... se fluye sin buscarlo. No obstante, el Oráculo también nos pone alerta: puesto que todo esto está provocado por algo externo a ti, inevitablemente depende de ese elemento catalizador, por lo tanto es inestable.

23. EL DESGASTE DEL TIEMPO

Si bien el amor aspira a ser eterno, una vez que nace está destinado a morir con el paso del tiempo, a pesar de nuestras mejores intenciones. El Oráculo indica la postura recomendada: mantente firme como una montaña, conserva una inmovilidad absoluta y déjate atravesar por lo que te sucede - también esto pasará.

24. UN NUEVO COMIENZO

Estás ante un nuevo comienzo. Prueba a preguntarte: «¿Dónde está la verdadera fuente luminosa que llamo amor?» De esta manera, gracias al impulso del amor, te acercarás a tu centro interior, y verás tu rostro original: esta llama íntima y profunda que habita en las entrañas de tu ser.

25. LA INOCENCIA DEL NIÑO

El hexagrama evoca el estado natural de las cosas. Es una invitación a actuar con naturalidad, precisamente como lo hace un niño: este es el auténtico comportamiento irreprochable.

26. EL MIEDO DEL AMOR

El Óraculo indica que estás disfrutando de una fuerza notable, por lo tanto es el momento adecuado para progresar. Aprovecha el estado actual de potencia para conseguir el valor de abandonarte totalmente...¡no retrocedas! Por miedo, muchos no arriesgan en el amor, conformándose con compromisos tibios.

27. EL ALIMENTO

Esta es la medida adecuada del amor: un alimento valioso, más que la comida, del cual el Oráculo aconseja no prescindir, si se quiere conservar un equilibrio psicofísico sano.

28. BAJO PRESIÓN

La situación es muy grave: las dificultades parecen insuperables. La situación en la que te encuentras es cuando menos desesperada. ¿Cómo salir de ella? Conserva una serenidad jovial. No importa cuan grande sea el peligro... ten confianza, este es el momento de apostar por tu corazón palpitante.

29. LA OSCURA NOCHE DEL ALMA

Estás viviendo el impacto con la angustia existencial que, por sorpresa, puede nublar la vida. El Oráculo indica la sencilla vía de escape: es necesario ir al meollo de las cosas y no detenerse en la superficie de los sucesos. En este sentido, el presagio es positivo: cualquiera que sea la oscuridad que te rodea, tienes capacidad para entender lo que desea enseñarte. ¡Aférrate a esa enseñanza!

30. EL ENAMORAMIENTO

El hexagrama encarna «la naturaleza en su esplendor», por lo tanto el Oráculo es sencillo: lo que estás viviendo eleva el corazón y el espíritu, y te pone en contacto con el esplendor perenne e imperecedero del amor. Deja arder totalmente esta llama, sin pretender nada más.

31. EL COMPROMISO
El Oráculo habla de unión de fuerzas esenciales, por lo que el presagio es feliz. Muéstrate receptivo a lo que sucede: ¡abandónate a lo que, simplemente, está sucediendo!

32. LA DURACIÓN
El Oráculo invita a evitar expresamente la rutina. Inmerso en la vida cotidiana, el amor muere por principio. La duración depende de una transformación perenne, y de una renovación continua.

33. EL ENGAÑO
Algo está haciendo que el amor desaparezca. De hecho esa energía se está retirando, se repliega sobre sí misma para protegerse: no puedes hacer nada más. En breve estarás exhausto. ¡Ya no verás ni rastro del amor!

34. CONFIANZA
El hexagrama indica el poder de la fuerza, la firmeza. Por lo tanto el Oráculo está diciendo que tienes la oportunidad de conseguir la auténtica grandeza: solo desde evolucionar de forma natural.

35. EL JUEGO DEL AMOR

El presagio es favorable: habla de expansión. Por fin has entendido que el amor es un juego... ya no hay nada en ti que le impida suceder.

36. OBSESIÓN (AVIDEZ)

La luz del amor se ve oscurecida por fuerzas primordiales o mentales que han tomado el control. Su naturaleza se ve ahogada u oscurecida por algo que impide su libre expresión como simple necesidad del alma. Procura intervenir en los condicionamientos que han ofuscado tu imaginación, tu capacidad de vivir fluidamente.

37. LA FAMILIA

Este hexagrama habla de la familia: es la voz de un hijo que lamenta la suerte de su madre, antaño una rama tierna y ahora convertida en ramita espinosa por el cansancio de criar a hijos ingratos. El Oráculo invita a ver el sentido del propio amor profundo, en el seno de la familia.

38. EL NO EN EL AMOR

Se trata de amor no correspondido. El Oráculo habla de diferencias irreconciliables, desunión, separación. Ambas voluntades en juego se expresan cada uno por su lado y no se encuentran, no se armonizan.

39. EL OBSTÁCULO

Un abismo terrorífico acompañado de una cumbre in-superable. Parece no que hay vía de escape: el peligro va a la par de la parálisis. Hay que encontrar una manera de vencer indirectamente estos obstáculos. ¿Qué puedo hacer? Es tiempo de medicación y conciencia.

40. LA LIBERACIÓN

El Oráculo indica una liberación verdadera, real, di-ferente de nuestra interpretación del término «libera-ción»: no es la negación del deseo, ni su consecución. Es observación a distancia y neutral.

41. EL SUFRIMIENTO

Tras a paso, cada placer se condensa, se endurece y se petrifica. El impulso alegre se reduce, es una ley na-tural. ¡También esto es vivir! Nos gustaría empaparnos solo de la alegría, pero el éxtasis sublime del amor des-encadena la agonía más atroz.

42. ÁMATE A TI MISMO

El Oráculo es una invitación concreta: ámate a ti mismo. ¡De hecho, el verdadero problema es que ni siquiera te aceptas! ¿Cuántas veces has hecho lo que realmente te apetecía? ¡Empieza aquí y ahora!

43. EL VALOR DEL AMOR

El Oráculo en sí es indefinido: es una mera advertencia. Si te empeñas en la negativa, obstaculizarás la fuerza del amor. Por el contrario, si esta fuerza asume en ti el sentido del valor -tanto de amar como de aceptar el amor- entonces...

44. EL ENCUENTRO ÍNTIMO

El Oráculo es una advertencia: si un encuentro tan íntimo y profundo está vinculado a mera seducción -del hombre o de la mujer- será una catástrofe segura.

45. LA FELICIDAD ES AMAR

Más allá de la mera realidad de pareja, el Oráculo habla de éxito, cuando se amplía la dimensión del amor a instrumento de cohesión con el consorcio humano. Hacerlo es sencillo: amar es suficiente.

46. EL SEXO

Al principio de la unión, el amor es sexualidad. Para evolucionar, hay que abandonarse al juego más sencillo del amor: esta es la invitación del Oráculo.

47. EL FRACASO

La pasión se acaba... pero la interpretación es delicada; no debes leerla de manera negativa: lo que está sucediendo es parte del ciclo de la vida. ¿Te sientes vacío?

No es *un mal*, al contrario, ha llegado la hora de hacer introspección: se acerca la temporada de la soledad. Aprender a bailar entre encuentros y separaciones.

48. EL MANANTIAL

La imagen representa lo más profundo del ser humano: evoca nuestra naturaleza esencial. El Oráculo es sencillo: no pierdas el contacto con ese interior íntimo, porque ahí aflora -de forma consciente o no- la fuerza vital que anima cada uno de tus gestos, toda tu vida.

49. LA TUMBA DEL AMOR

En el matrimonio existe una represión, una domesticación del amor en función de otros intereses, de miedos primarios de uno mismo, que lo abocan a su fin. El Oráculo señala que es momento de revolución: piensa en qué se basa tu vida. Te invita a regenerarte: en ti existe una fuerza creadora capaz de renovar y de renovarte constantemente.

50. EL CRISOL

El Oráculo te invita a basar tu amor en la dimensión de la honestidad y de la sinceridad: puedes hacerlo, usando tu energía para no depender de tu pareja en tu supervivencia....¡a todos los niveles!

51. EL SUCESO FATAL

El Oráculo te aconseja que vivas este momento de intensidad tal como es: dejará una huella íntima y perenne en tu vida. Entra en profundidad en el instante presente: siente el temblor, escucha ese escalofrío, deja que el corazón hable al corazón. Sucede.... solo debes eliminar cualquier obstáculo para que suceda. Solo así el amor sigue recreándose.

52. EL TESTIGO

Si estás en un estado de turbación, si el amor te está destrozando con sus giros inesperados... ¡crea en ti un espacio de paz en el que resguardarte!

53. LA INTIMIDAD

La dimensión en la que el Oráculo habla no es la esfera de las certezas, de la posesión y de los celos. La intimidad, que es la montaña invisible del amor, se basa en algo que ninguno de nuestros cinco sentidos puede captar. No es más que vacío y silencio.

54. LA JOVEN ESPOSA

Aquí se representan todas las relaciones libres entre seres humanos. Para el I Ching la fuerza del amor es tal que borra y elimina cualquier convención y cualquier regla establecida por las normas sociales. El Oráculo habla de la armonía superior que el amor provoca en el mundo.

55. LA PLENITUD

Para el Oráculo este es un momento de plenitud: el fuego ardiente de la fuerza vital irrumpe con el fragor de un rayo, anulándose y anulando cualquier inhibición de la conciencia. Desaparece cualquier sentido de apatía: estás ante una experiencia vital. Tal vez la percibes como una muerte del yo, pero no tengas miedo: ¡por primera vez... estás viviendo!

56. EL CAMINANTE

El presagio habla al caminante que hay en ti. Al pasar de una experiencia a otra, al encontrar a amigos y amantes, eres un caminante. Algo te impide detenerte para siempre: lo intentas y lo vuelves a intentar, y cada vez crees haber conseguido un morada estable. Pero llega un momento, y es este, en el que sientes que debes retomar el camino.

57. EL VIENTO

El Oráculo invita a observar la existencia: todo lo que te sucede, cada cosa, obsérvalo *directamente*... como meros hechos desnudos y crudos, sin etiquetas, sin decir si es correcto o incorrecto, bueno o malo. Deja a un lado la mente y su perenne juicio.

58. EL AMISTAD

Es la comunicación fluida entre dos seres que se compenetran...¡sin penetrarse! El Oráculo indica que, sin vosotros quererlo, gracias a la intimidad, la relación que tienes con tu pareja se ha transformado en amistad.

59. LA SOLEDAD

El Oráculo invita a sumergirse plenamente en el propio ser. Esta carta marca el límite de las infinitas experiencias del mundo exterior e indica el camino a seguir para seguir evolucionando. En el culmen de tantas esperanzas, eliminado el egoísmo -la idea de ser un pequeño yo separado y en lucha contra todo y contra todos- nos encontramos solos. ¡En la unión íntima que es la esencia de la vida, estamos solos!

60. LA LIMITACIÓN

El hexagrama advierte: estableciendo límites demasiado rígidos al amor se coarta su libertad y que fluya libremente, se obstaculiza la evolución constante.

61. EL MOMENTO PRESENTE

El hexagrama ofrece la imagen de un corazón libre, capaz de percibir lo Verdadero y de aferrarlo. El Oráculo es una invitación a sumergirse en la propia verdad presente: vive «aquí y ahora» – en el tiempo real en el que habita toda la existencia.

62. LAS IDENTIFICACIONES

El Oráculo advierte: ¡presta atención a las identificaciones! Ciertamente, el amor aporta una plenitud y una dicha sin igual, pero si se identifica esa plenitud con una persona, nos abrimos a espacios de dolor y de desgracia inmensos, sometiéndonos nosotros mismos y al otro a una pesadísima esclavitud o dependencia.

63. LA TRANSFIGURACIÓN

Todo alcanza la plenitud, la completa resolución, transforma y pone en contacto con la dimensión del espíritu... es un momento, que encierra en sí los indicios de la decadencia. Sumérgete y vive al máximo en esta dimensión, antes de que se convierta en un recuerdo, una ilusión, un sueño.

64. LA UNIÓN MÍSTICA

El Oráculo habla de un encuentro fallido; se anhela algo, se espera, pero la fusión no se produce. Es una advertencia: en la íntima comunión generada por el amor con un amante, se llega a captar la posible *Unión mística* que es plenitud y realización. Es un relámpago de intuición precioso, pero inefable; por eso es fundamental unir amor y meditación.

LE YI JING DE L'AMOUR

MÉTHODE DE TIRAGE SIMPLIFIÉE

Trouvez un moment pour être seul avec vous-même, dans un endroit isolé, loin du stress et du bruit. Détendez-vous simplement en écoutant votre souffle et, lorsque vous sentez que vous pouvez entrer en contact avec votre Moi le plus intime, mélangez les cartes: les 64 hexagrammes traditionnels du *Yi Jing* (Livre des mutations) ont été considérés du point de vue de l'amour et traduits en images pour rendre leur impact plus immédiat. Visualisez intérieurement votre expérience actuelle de l'amour: laissez-la émerger devant vous pour ce qu'elle est, ne la jugez pas, ne l'interprétez pas, n'aspirez pas à quelque chose de différent; il n'est nécessaire de poser aucune question. N'oubliez pas: vous ne recherchez pas une consolation, vous ne voulez pas non plus modifier ce qui vous arrive: vous voulez simplement comprendre. Lorsque vous vous sentez prêt, disposez le jeu et, de la main gauche, retournez une carte: lisez la description et observez l'image en essayant de comprendre la façon dont elle éclaircit votre situation.

Fermez les yeux et méditez sur le message en silence. L'acceptation est la première clé de lecture, car elle est en mesure de produire un changement, mais elle est surtout capable de vous aider à voir de façon détachée l'expérience que la vie vous offre... et n'oubliez pas: cette phase aussi passera, ce n'est qu'une saison de votre vie. Par conséquent, accueillez en vous ce que la carte vous suggère, sans vous abattre ni vous exalter. C'est la leçon fondamentale du *Yi Jing de l'amour.*

LES JUGEMENTS

1. LE DÉSIR CRÉATIF

La tradition orientale voit dans le désir le début de l'univers. Cette carte est une invitation à ne pas se compliquer la vie: *acceptez le désir.* Ce n'est pas bien de lutter contre la sexualité. Toute répression vous mettra en lutte contre vous-même... et pour atteindre votre plein épanouissement, vous avez besoin de toutes vos forces. Cette carte indique que vous êtes en harmonie avec le pouvoir créatif de l'univers.

2. LA RÉCEPTIVITÉ

Cette carte est un signe de forte présence du *Yin*, c'est-à-dire de réceptivité, dans votre vie. Observez la façon dont il vous gouverne, ce qu'il implique et ce qui en découle: la force créatrice s'installe en vous et se concrétise.

3. LA DIFFICULTÉ INITIALE
L'Oracle invite à ne pas réduire l'autre à un objet d'usage, ni à se vendre au nom de l'amour, mais plutôt à s'abandonner au magnétisme cosmique qui se crée dans l'amour.

4. L'INEXPÉRIENCE DES JEUNES
L'Oracle vous indique que vous vous trouvez au bord d'un gouffre, mais ne vous inquiétez pas: la nature insouciante de cette carte vous fait voler, surmontant ainsi tout obstacle qui vous empêche de progresser.

5. L'ATTENTE
En amour, il est important de laisser l'amour se réaliser. L'attente est un enchantement... Pendant un moment, vous entrez en contact avec votre propre essence et vous vous y recueillez. L'Oracle dit que vous êtes en attente. Ne désirez rien d'autre!

6. LE CONFLIT
Nous colorons généralement l'amour de rêves et d'imagination, de prétentions et de croyances, nous l'empêchons ainsi d'exister ou le conditionnons au point de

le déformer. Est-ce votre cas? Regardez comment vous avez manipulé votre amour.

7. LA COHÉSION

Dans toutes les réalités de la vie, et surtout en amour, mieux vaut avoir en soi un point de cohésion. Toute rencontre sera ainsi un partage et vous permettra de vous enrichir et de vous épanouir au contact de l'autre. Recentrez-vous en vous-même!

8. LA SOLIDARITÉ DES COMPLÉMENTAIRES

Le Tao se dédouble pour se manifester. C'est l'alternance continue de repos et de mouvement qui crée la vie: un jeu de causes et d'effets derrière lequel il existe quelque chose de perpétuellement immobile. La sagesse, c'est arriver à percevoir ce point de quiétude absolue présent en nous: l'œil du cyclone.

9. L'IMPUISSANCE

Vous êtes dépassé par les événements; vous ne pouvez rien faire pour que la situation évolue, vous ne pouvez provoquer aucun changement. Acceptez cette impuissance. Cela aussi c'est de l'amour.

10. VOTRE GUIDE INTÉRIEUR

L'Oracle vous rappelle que vous avez en vous un guide capable de vous enraciner dans le bonheur, pourtant vous ne l'utilisez pas; vous n'en êtes même pas conscient! Ne vous inquiétez pas: il peut être revitalisé, il doit même être réveillé si vous voulez vivre l'amour dans toute sa plénitude.

11. L'HARMONIE: AMOUR ET PAIX

Dans toute fusion d'amour, on se retrouve plongé dans la plénitude du présent: c'est là que se concentre le bonheur total. Permettez-vous de vous perdre dans la brièveté de cet instant, dans les bras de votre bien-aimé(e). N'en demandez pas plus!

12. LA SUPERFICIALITÉ

Ne nous leurrons pas: nous aimons pour les raisons les plus diverses et elles aboutissent toutes à la stagnation. Le *Yi Jing* vous conseille de vous replier sur vous-même, dans votre intimité secrète, pour donner de la profondeur à l'amour.

13. ÊTRE AMOUREUX

Tout amour renferme un message d'ouverture qui n'est pas celui d'imposer sa volonté, mais de transmettre plutôt le sens et la vibration d'être en harmonie avec la force universelle qui gouverne toute l'existence. L'amour est une puissance en soi et pour soi, il ne s'impose pas: il se limite au partage.

14. LA TOTALITÉ

Les temps sont favorables: vous avez une maîtrise de la vie qui vous permet une totale liberté d'action. Et le fait que vous ne fassiez rien pour que cette harmonie se concrétise montre que ce n'est pas de l'égoïsme.

15. L'UNICITÉ

Quand l'amour arrive, il ne se voit pas de manière éclatante: il se révèle dans une image de modestie que l'hexagramme illustre comme «la montagne, en bas» qui se cache «sur la terre, en haut». L'Oracle est un présage favorable.

16. LA FERVEUR

L'Oracle témoigne de l'heureux élan de force qui devient, une fois partagé, de la ferveur. Le succès vient du fait de s'abandonner au pouvoir de l'amour: l'absence de résistance est la seule chose requise.

17. SE REGARDER

L'Oracle parle de quelque chose qui survient «en se regardant». Le sens est simple: l'acceptation de la situation. Dans cette harmonie, qui n'est ni condescendance ni compromis, on participe au rythme naturel du monde.

18. PRENDRE CONSCIENCE

L'hexagramme décrit une situation statique. L'Oracle ne veut pas juger cet état des choses, il nous invite plutôt à réfléchir sur les mécanismes ou les conditionnements qui la génèrent, et sur les qualités intérieures à focaliser pour sortir d'une situation de stagnation dans laquelle on ne peut que pourrir.

19. S'ÉCOUTER

L'Oracle donne un présage de prospérité. Vous évoluez dans une situation qui mûrit, jour après jour, et porte ses fruits.

20. LA CONTEMPLATION

Dans son ensemble, au sein de la doctrine taoïste, cet hexagramme représente la vision du monde du sage: *Kuan* est une attention sans objet, non limitée par l'ego. Concrètement, c'est la méditation... l'autre visage de l'amour: apprenez à l'inclure dans votre vie quotidienne.

21. SE TRAHIR (LA JALOUSIE)

Vous êtes en train de vivre le côté obscur de l'amour? Accordez-vous le temps d'assimiler la trahison. Dans ces moments de désespoir, ce que nous aimions chez l'autre apparaît avec une certitude absolue: observez-le et faites-le vôtre, en gardant votre conscience en vous. Dans cette présence attentive, murissez et évoluez: devenez vous-même.

22. SE TOUCHER

En apparence, l'Oracle est favorable. Pendant un moment, on vit dans une dimension libre de toute inquiétude… on avance insouciant malgré soi. Mais l'Oracle nous met également en garde: puisque ceci est causé par quelque chose d'externe à vous, tout dépend inévitablement de cet élément catalyseur, d'où l'instabilité de la situation.

23. L'USURE DU TEMPS

Bien que l'amour s'ouvre à quelque chose d'éternel, puisqu'il naît dans le temps, il est destiné à périr malgré les meilleures intentions. L'Oracle indique l'attitude à adopter: soyez solide comme une montagne, gardez une immobilité absolue et laissez-vous traverser par ce qui vous arrive - cela aussi passera.

24. UN NOUVEAU DÉPART

Un nouveau départ vous attend. Essayez de vous demander: «Où est la véritable source de lumière que j'appelle l'amour? ». Ainsi, grâce à l'impulsion de l'amour, vous vous approcherez de votre centre intérieur et vous verrez votre vrai visage: cette flamme intime et profonde qui habite dans les profondeurs de votre âme.

25. L'INNOCENCE DE L'ENFANT

L'hexagramme évoque l'état naturel des choses. C'est une invitation à agir naturellement, comme le fait un enfant: c'est le vrai comportement irréprochable.

26. LA PEUR DE L'AMOUR

L'Oracle indique que vous jouissez d'une force considérable. Le moment est donc propice pour progresser. Tirez le courage de votre état actuel de puissance pour vous abandonner totalement... ne vous rétractez pas! Par peur, beaucoup n'osent pas trop s'investir dans l'amour, se contentant de maigres compromis.

27. LE NUTRIMENT

C'est la bonne mesure de l'amour: un nutriment précieux, plus que la nourriture, auquel l'Oracle nous recommande de pourvoir, si l'on veut maintenir un bon équilibre psychophysique.

28. SOUS PRESSION

La situation est très grave: les difficultés semblent insurmontables. La position dans laquelle vous vous trouvez est pour le moins désespérée. Comment s'en sortir? Gardez une sérénité joyeuse. Peu importe la gravité du danger... soyez confiant, le moment est venu de vous concentrer sur votre cœur qui bat.

29. LA NUIT SOMBRE DE L'ÂME

Vous vivez l'impact avec l'angoisse existentielle qui peut, à l'improviste, obscurcir la vie. L'Oracle trace le chemin le plus simple vers l'issue: vous devez aller au cœur des choses et ne pas vous arrêter à la surface des événements. En ce sens, le présage est positif: quelle que soit l'obscurité dans laquelle vous êtes plongé, il existe en vous une conscience à même de saisir son enseignement. Accrochez-vous à elle!

30. TOMBER AMOUREUX

L'hexagramme incarne «la nature dans toute sa splendeur», l'Oracle est donc simple: ce que vous vivez élève le cœur et l'esprit et vous met en contact avec la splendeur éternelle et impérissable de l'amour. Laissez cette flamme brûler complètement, sans rien prétendre d'autre.

31. LES FIANÇAILLES

L'Oracle parle de l'union des forces essentielles, le présage est donc heureux. Soyez réceptif à ce qui se passe: abandonnez-vous à ce qui vous arrive tout simplement!

32. LA DURÉE

L'Oracle invite à éviter expressément la routine. Plongé dans la vie quotidienne, l'amour meurt d'emblée. La durée est déterminée par une transformation perpétuelle, et donc par un renouvellement continu.

33. LA DUPERIE

Quelque chose met l'amour en fuite. En fait, cette énergie s'atténue peu à peu, elle se replie sur elle-même pour se protéger: elle ne peut pas faire autrement. Bref, vous serez épuisé et vous ne verrez même plus l'ombre de cet amour!

34. LA CONFIANCE

L'hexagramme indique le pouvoir de la force, de la fermeté. Ainsi, l'Oracle dit que vous avez la possibilité d'atteindre la vraie grandeur: il vous suffit d'évoluer naturellement.

35. LE JEU DE L'AMOUR

Le présage est favorable: il parle de progression. Enfin, vous avez compris que l'amour est un jeu… rien en vous ne l'empêche plus d'arriver.

36. L'OBSESSION (AVIDITÉ)

La lumière de l'amour est obscurcie par des forces primordiales ou mentales qui ont pris le dessus. Son naturel est étouffé ou obscurci par quelque chose qui l'empêche d'exprimer librement le simple besoin de l'âme. Veillez à intervenir sur les conditionnements qui ont assombri votre imagination, votre capacité à vivre de manière fluide.

37. LA FAMILLE

Cet hexagramme parle de la famille: c'est la voix d'un fils qui se plaint du sort de sa mère, autrefois tendre rameau, aujourd'hui fagot épineux à force d'élever des enfants ingrats. L'Oracle nous invite à voir le sens de notre amour profond au sein de la famille.

38. LE NON EN AMOUR

C'est l'amour non partagé. L'Oracle parle de diversités infranchissables, de désunion, de séparation. Les deux volontés en jeu s'expriment individuellement et ne se rencontrent pas, elles ne s'harmonisent pas.

39. L'OBSTACLE

Un abîme terrifiant est accompagné d'un sommet insurmontable. Il semble n'y avoir aucune issue: le danger est accompagné de la paralysie. Il faut trouver un moyen de surmonter indirectement ces obstacles. Que faire? Il est temps de méditer et de prendre conscience.

40. LA LIBÉRATION

L'Oracle indique une véritable libération, réelle, différente de notre interprétation du terme «libération»: ce n'est pas la négation du désir, ni son accomplissement. C'est l'observation détachée et neutre.

41. LA SOUFFRANCE

Petit à petit, tout plaisir se condense, se raidit, se pétrifie. La pulsion joyeuse s'atténue, c'est une loi naturelle. Cela aussi c'est vivre! Nous voudrions ne capturer que la joie, mais c'est l'extase sublime de l'amour qui déclenche l'agonie la plus atroce.

42. AIMEZ-VOUS

L'Oracle est une invitation spécifique: aimez-vous. En fait, le vrai problème est que, souvent, vous ne vous acceptez pas! Combien de fois avez-vous fait ce qui vous a procuré un réel plaisir? Commencez maintenant, ici, tout de suite!

43. LE COURAGE DE L'AMOUR

L'Oracle en soi est indéfini: c'est un simple avertissement. Si vous vous obstinez à refuser, la force de l'amour sera entravée. Inversement, si cette force assume en vous le sens du courage - que ce soit le courage d'aimer ou d'accepter l'amour - alors...

44. LA RENCONTRE INTIME

L'Oracle est un avertissement: si une rencontre aussi intime et profonde est liée à la simple séduction - d'un homme ou d'une femme - une catastrophe s'ensuivra.

45. LE BONHEUR C'EST AIMER

Au-delà de la simple réalité du couple, l'Oracle parle de réussite, lorsque la dimension de l'amour s'étend à un outil de cohésion avec l'humanité. C'est simple: il suffit d'aimer.

46. LE SEXE

Au début de l'union, l'amour c'est la sexualité. Pour évoluer, il faut s'abandonner au jeu plus simple de l'amour: telle est l'invitation de l'Oracle.

47. L'ÉCHEC

Toute passion finit par s'éteindre... mais l'interprétation est délicate; elle ne doit pas être lue de manière négative: ce qui se passe fait partie du cycle de la vie. Vous sentez-vous vide, vidé? Ce n'est pas *une mauvaise chose*, au contraire, il est temps de revenir à soi-même: la saison de la solitude approche. Apprenez à danser entre les rencontres et les séparations.

48. LA SOURCE

L'image décrit ce qu'il y a de plus profond en nous, les humains: elle évoque notre nature essentielle. L'Oracle est simple: ne perdez pas le contact avec cette intériorité intime, car c'est à partir de là qu'émerge, consciemment ou non, la force vitale qui anime chacun de vos gestes, toute votre vie.

49. LA TOMBE DE L'AMOUR

Le mariage, c'est la répression, la domestication de l'amour en fonction d'autres intérêts, des peurs primordiales du Moi, qui finissent par en décréter la fin. L'Oracle indique qu'il est temps d'opérer une révolution: évaluez les aspects sur lesquels se base votre vie. L'invitation est de vous régénérer: il existe en vous une force créatrice capable de renouveler et de vous renouveler perpétuellement.

50. LE CREUSET

L'Oracle est une invitation à enraciner votre amour dans la dimension de l'honnêteté et de la sincérité: vous pouvez le faire en utilisant votre énergie pour ne pas dépendre de votre partenaire pour votre survie... à tous les niveaux!

51. L'ÉVÉNEMENT FATAL

Le conseil de l'Oracle est de vivre ce moment d'intensité pour ce qu'il est: il laissera une trace intime et permanente dans votre vie. Entrez profondément dans l'instant présent: sentez-vous frémir, écoutez ce frisson, laissez le cœur parler au cœur. Cela se produit... il faut simplement éliminer tout ce qui entrave sa réalisation. C'est seulement de cette manière que l'amour continue à se recréer.

52. LE TÉMOIN

Si votre esprit est en émoi, si l'amour vous bouleverse avec son tourbillonnement... créez en vous un espace de calme où vous pourrez vous accorder une pause!

53. L'INTIMITÉ

La dimension dans laquelle l'Oracle parle n'est pas la sphère de la sécurité, de la possession et de la jalousie. L'intimité, qui est la montagne invisible de l'amour, plonge ses racines dans quelque chose qui ne peut être saisi par aucun des cinq sens. Ce n'est que vide et silence.

54. LA JEUNE MARIÉE

Toutes les relations libres entre les êtres humains sont décrites ici. Pour le *Yi Jing*, la force de l'amour est telle qu'elle brise et élimine toutes les conventions et toutes les règles établies par les normes sociales. L'Oracle parle de l'harmonie supérieure que l'amour crée dans le monde.

55. LA PLÉNITUDE

Pour l'Oracle, c'est un moment de plénitude: le feu brûlant de la force vitale éclate comme un coup de tonnerre, s'évanouit annulant toute inhibition de la conscience. Toute sensation d'apathie a disparu: vous affrontez une expérience vitale. Peut-être la percevez-vous comme une mort du Moi, mais n'ayez crainte: pour la première fois... vous vivez!

56. LE VOYAGEUR

Le présage parle au voyageur qui est en vous. En passant d'une expérience à l'autre, en rencontrant des amis et des amants, vous êtes devenu un voyageur. Quelque chose vous empêche de vous arrêter une bonne fois pour toutes: vous essayez encore et encore et à chaque fois vous pensez avoir atteint un foyer stable. Mais il arrive un moment, et c'est maintenant, où vous sentez que vous devez reprendre votre chemin.

57. LE VENT

L'Oracle vous invite à considérer l'existence: tout ce qui vous arrive, tout chose, observez-la *directement...* comme de simples faits, sans étiquette, sans dire que cela est juste ou injuste, bon ou mauvais. Laissez de côté l'esprit et son jugement constant.

58. L'AMITIÉ

C'est une communication fluide entre deux êtres qui s'interpénètrent... sans se pénétrer! L'Oracle indique que malgré vous, grâce à l'intimité, la relation que vous entretenez avec votre partenaire s'est transformée en amitié.

59. LA SOLITUDE

L'Oracle vous invite à vous immerger complètement dans votre être. Cette carte marque la fin des nombreuses expériences dans le monde extérieur et indique la voie à suivre pour mener à bien une évolution ultérieure. Au sommet de tant d'expériences, après avoir chassé l'égoïsme - l'idée d'être un petit Moi séparé et luttant contre toute chose et tout le monde - nous nous retrouvons seuls. Dans l'union intime qui est l'essence de la vie, on est seul!

60. LA LIMITATION

L'hexagramme avertit: en imposant des limites trop sévères à l'amour, vous empêchez sa liberté et son cours, entravant ainsi son évolution constante.

61. LE MOMENT PRÉSENT

L'hexagramme offre l'image d'un cœur libre, capable de percevoir le Vrai et de l'accueillir en lui-même. L'Oracle est une invitation à se plonger dans sa vérité présente: vivre *«ici et maintenant»* - en temps réel où toute l'existence demeure!

62. LES IDENTIFICATIONS

L'Oracle avertit: faites attention aux identifications! Certes, l'amour conduit à une plénitude et à une béatitude sans égales, mais si l'on identifie cette plénitude à une personne, se manifestent alors une douleur et un malheur immenses qui obligent l'un et l'autre à se soumettre à un esclavage accablant ou à une forte dépendance.

63. LA TRANSFIGURATION

Tout chose aboutit à la plénitude, à la résolution complète, elle transfigure et met en contact avec la dimension de l'esprit... c'est un court instant qui cache les signes de la décadence. Abandonnez-vous et vivez autant que vous pouvez dans cette dimension, avant que cela ne devienne un souvenir, une illusion, un rêve.

64. L'UNION MYSTIQUE

L'Oracle parle d'une rencontre manquée; on aspire à quelque chose, on espère, mais la fusion ne se produit pas. C'est un avertissement: dans la communion intime générée par l'amour avec l'être aimé, on arrive à saisir l'*Union mystique* possible qui est l'achèvement et l'épanouissement. C'est un éclair d'intuition précieux mais ineffable - pour cela, il est essentiel d'unir l'amour à la méditation.

I CHING
DO AMOR

MÉTODO DE LEITURA SIMPLIFICADO

Encontre um momento para ficar consigo mesmo, em um ambiente isolado, livre de distrações habituais. Relaxe-se simplesmente sentindo a respiração e, quando perceber que pode entrar em contato com o seu eu mais íntimo, misture as cartas: os 64 hexagramas tradicionais do *I Ching* (Livro das Alterações) foram lidos em termos de amor e traduzidos em imagens que tornam seu impacto mais imediato. Visualize interiormente a sua experiência atual do amor: deixe-a emergir à sua frente pelo que isso representa, não a julgue, não a interprete, não a queira diferente; e não é necessário registrar nenhuma pergunta. Lembre-se: você não esta procurando consolações, nem quer mudar o que lhe está acontecendo: você quer entender. Quando estiver pronto, espalhe o baralho e, com a mão esquerda, vire uma carta: leia a descrição e contemple a imagem, observando como ela lança luz sobre o seu estado de coisas. Feche os olhos e pondere silenciosamente sobre a mensagem. A aceitação é a primeira chave da leitura, porque é capaz de produzir uma mudança, mas, acima de tudo, é capaz de ajudá-lo a ver de maneira desapegada a experiência que a vida está lhe oferecendo... e lembre-se: isso também passará, é apenas um período da sua vida. Portanto, aceite para você mesmo aquilo que a carta sugere, sem desanimar-se ou exaltar-se. Esta é a lição fundamental do I Ching do Amor.

OS JULGAMENTOS

1. O DESEJO CRIATIVO
A tradição oriental vê no desejo o começo do universo. Esta carta é um convite para não complicar a sua vida: *aceite o desejo*. Não é bom lutar contra a sexualidade. Toda repressão o colocará em luta contra si mesmo... e para alcançar a plena realização, você precisa de todas as suas forças. A carta indica que você está em sintonia com o poder criativo do universo.

2. A RECEPTIVIDADE
Esta carta é um sinal de forte presença *Yin*, isto é, de receptividade, em sua vida. Observe como ela o governa, o que isso implica e o que deriva dela: a força criativa está se estabelecendo em você e adquirindo concretude.

3. A DIFICULDADE INICIAL

O Oráculo oferece um convite para que a outra pessoa não fique reduzida a um objeto que se usa comumente, nem se vender em nome do amor, mas sim render-se ao magnetismo cósmico que se ativa no amor.

4. A INEXPERIÊNCIA JUVENIL

O Oráculo está lhe dizendo que você está em frente de um abismo, mas não se preocupe: por necessidade, a despreocupação que caracteriza esta carta o leva a fluir, superando assim qualquer obstáculo que o impeça de progredir.

5. A ESPERA

No amor, é importante deixar que o amor em si seja realizado. A espera é um encanto ... Por um momento, você entra em contato com sua própria essência e se reúne nela. O Oráculo diz que você está esperando. Não querer mais nada!

6. O CONFLITO

Geralmente colorimos o amor de sonhos e fantasias, de pretensões e crenças, impedindo-o de existir ou condicionando-o a ponto de deformá-lo. Esse é o seu caso? Veja como você manipulou seu amor.

7. A COESÃO

Em todas as realidades da vida, e acima de tudo no amor, é bom ter um ponto de coesão; portanto, qualquer encontro será um compartilhamento e você poderá enriquecer a si mesmo e expandir o contato com o outro. Volte a centralizar-se em si mesmo!

8. SOLIDARIEDADE DOS COMPLEMENTOS

O Tao, para se manifestar, se duplica. É a alternância contínua de descanso e movimento que cria a vida: um jogo de causas e efeitos, por trás do qual há algo perpetuamente imóvel. A sabedoria é perceber esse ponto de absoluta tranquilidade presente em nós: o olho do ciclone.

9. A IMPOTÊNCIA

Você está assoberbado pelos eventos: você não pode fazer nada para fazer com que a situação evolua, nem pode causar qualquer mudança. Aceite essa impotência. Isso também é amor.

10. O SEU GUIA INTERNO

O Oráculo lembra que dentro de você existe um guia que pode enraizá-lo na felicidade, mas você não o usa; você nem está até mesmo ciente disso! Não se preocupe: ele pode ser revitalizado; de fato, deve ser despertado, se você deseja viver a plenitude do amor.

11. A HARMONIA: AMOR E PAZ

Em cada uma das fusões do amor, você se encontra imerso na plenitude do presente: nela está a realização total. Permita-se perder-se na brevidade deste momento, nos braços de sua amada. Não pedir mais nada!

12. A SUPERFICIALIDADE

Não nos iludamos: facilmente, amamos pelas mais diversas razões e todas levam à estagnação. O I Ching aconselha você a se retirar, na sua intimidade secreta, a dar profundidade ao amor.

13. ESTAR APAIXONADO

Qualquer amor tem em si uma mensagem de abertura, que não é impor a própria vontade, mas transmitir o significado e a vibração de estar em harmonia com a força universal que governa toda a existência. O amor é poder em si mesmo, não se impõe: limita-se a compartilhar.

14. A TOTALIDADE

Os tempos são favoráveis: você tem um domínio da vida que permite total liberdade de ação. A demonstração que não é egoísmo se deduz do fato que você não faz nada a fim que essa harmonia aconteça.

15. A UNICIDADE

O amor acontece e não é nada vistoso: revela-se numa imagem de modéstia que o hexagrama ilustra como "a montanha, embaixo", que se esconde "na terra, em cima". O Oráculo é um presságio favorável.

16. O FERVOR

O Oráculo testemunha o feliz ímpeto da força que, uma vez compartilhada, se torna fervorosa. O sucesso é dado abandonando-se ao poder do amor: a ausência de resistência é a única coisa necessária.

17. OLHAR-SE

O Oráculo fala sobre algo que está acontecendo "olhando-se". O significado é simples: aceitação do estado das coisas. Nisso harmonizar-se, que não é condescendente nem requer compromissos, participa-se do ritmo natural do mundo.

18. TORNAR-SE CONSCIENTE

O hexagrama representa uma situação estática. O Oráculo não quer julgar esse estado de coisas, mas nos convida a refletir sobre os mecanismos ou condicionamentos que o geram, e sobre as qualidades internas a serem focadas para sair de uma situação de estagnação na qual só se pode apodrecer.

19. OUVIR-SE

O Oráculo dá um presságio de prosperidade. Você está evoluindo dentro de uma situação que, dia após dia, amadurece e dá frutos.

20. A CONTEMPLAÇÃO

Como um todo, dentro da doutrina taoísta, esse hexagrama representa a visão do mundo do sábio: *Kuan* é atenção sem um objeto, não limitado pelo ego. Na prática, é meditação... a outra face do amor: aprenda a incluí-la em sua vida diária.

21. TRAIR-SE (O CIÚME)

Você está experimentando o lado sombrio do amor? Permita-se tempo para assimilar a traição. Nesses momentos de desespero, o que amamos no outro aparece com absoluta certeza: observe-o e torne-o seu, mantendo sua consciência em você. Nesta presença atenta, cresça e evolua: torne-se você mesmo.

22. TOCAR-SE

Aparentemente, o Oráculo é favorável. Por um momento, você se vê vivendo em uma dimensão livre de qualquer ansiedade... ela flui contra a nossa vontade. No entanto, o Oráculo também adverte: como tudo isso é causado por algo externo a você, depende inevitavelmente daquele elemento catalisador, portanto é instável.

23. O DESGASTE DO TEMPO

Embora o amor se abra para algo eterno, uma vez que nasce no tempo, ele está destinado a perecer, apesar das melhores intenções. O Oráculo indica a atitude a adotar: permaneça firme como uma montanha, mantenha uma imobilidade absoluta e deixe-se atravessar pelo que acontece com você - isso também passará.

24. UM INÍCIO NOVO

Você está enfrentando um novo início. Tente se perguntar: "Onde está a verdadeira fonte de luz que chamo de amor?" Dessa maneira, graças ao impulso do amor, você se aproximará do seu centro interior e verá sua face original: aquela chama íntima e profunda que habita nas profundezas do seu ser.

25. A INOCÊNCIA DA CRIANÇA

O hexagrama evoca o estado natural das coisas. É um convite para agir naturalmente, assim como uma criança: esse é o verdadeiro comportamento irrepreensível.

26. O MEDO DO AMOR

O Oráculo indica que você está desfrutando de uma força considerável; portanto, é o momento certo para progredir. Tome a coragem do seu atual estado de poder para se abandonar totalmente... não se afaste! Por medo, muitos não se atrevem em amor, contentando-se com compromissos monótonos.

27. A NUTRIÇÃO

Esta é a medida certa do amor: uma nutrição preciosa, mais do que a comida, que o Oráculo recomenda não deixar que falte, se quisermos manter um equilíbrio psicofísico saudável.

28. SOB PRESSÃO

A situação é muito séria: as dificuldades parecem intransponíveis. A posição em que você está é por assim dizer desesperada. Como sair disso? Mantenha uma serenidade alegre. Não importa quão sério seja o perigo... enraíze-se na confiança, este é o momento para se concentrar no seu coração palpitante.

29. A NOITE ESCURA DA ALMA

Você está experimentando o impacto da angústia existencial que pode, repentinamente, obscurecer a vida. O Oráculo traça a saída mais simples: você precisa ir ao cerne das coisas e não parar na superfície dos eventos. Nesse sentido, o presságio é positivo: seja qual for a escuridão em que você está imerso, há em você a consciência que é capaz de compreender seus ensinamentos. Ancore-se nisso!

30. A PAIXÃO

O hexagrama incorpora "a natureza em seu esplendor"; portanto, o Oráculo é simples: o que você está experimentando eleva o coração e o espírito e coloca você em contato com o esplendor eterno e perene do amor. Deixe essa chama queimar totalmente, sem esperar por mais nada.

31. O NOIVADO

O Oráculo fala da união de forças essenciais, portanto, o presságio é feliz. Seja receptivo ao que acontece: abandone-se ao que está simplesmente acontecendo!

32. A DURAÇÃO

O Oráculo pede que se evite expressamente a rotina. Imerso na vida cotidiana, o amor morre em um estágio inicial. A duração é dada por uma transformação perene e, portanto, por uma renovação contínua.

33. O ENGANO

Algo está afastando o amor. De fato, essa energia está recuando, voltando a se proteger: não pode fazer de outra maneira. Em resumo, você estará exausto e nunca mais verá nem menos a sombra do amor!

34. CONFIANÇA

O hexagrama indica o poder da força, firmeza. Portanto, o Oráculo está dizendo que você tem a oportunidade de alcançar a verdadeira grandeza: você só precisa evoluir-se naturalmente

35. O JOGO DO AMOR

O presságio é favorável: fala de expansão. Finalmente, você entendeu que o amor é um jogo... nada em você impede que isso aconteça mais.

36. OBSESSÃO (GANÂNCIA)

A luz do amor é obscurecida por forças primordiais ou mentais que assumiram o controle. A sua naturalidade é sufocada ou obscurecida por algo que impede sua livre expressão de uma simples necessidade da alma. Procure intervir nos condicionamentos que embaçaram a sua imaginação, a sua capacidade de viver fluidamente.

37. A FAMÍLIA

Esse hexagrama fala da família: é a voz de um filho que lamenta o destino de sua mãe, antes um ramo delicado, que agora se tornou um faixo espinhoso pelo esforço de criar filhos ingratos. O Oráculo nos convida a ver o significado de nosso próprio amor profundo dentro da família.

38. O NÃO NO AMOR

É amor não correspondido. O Oráculo fala de diversidade intransponível, desunião e separação. As duas vontades do jogo se expressam cada uma por si mesma e não se encontram, não se harmonizam.

39. O OBSTÁCULO

Um abismo aterrorizante é acompanhado por um pico intransponível. Parece não haver saída: o perigo é acompanhado por paralisia. Precisamos encontrar uma maneira de superar indiretamente esses obstáculos. O que fazer? É hora de meditação e conscientização.

40. A LIBERTAÇÃO

O Oráculo indica uma libertação verdadeira, real, diferente da nossa interpretação do termo "libertação": não é a negação do desejo, nem a sua realização. É uma observação imparcial e neutra.

41. O SOFRIMENTO

Passo a passo, todo prazer se condensa, se endurece, se petrifica. O impulso alegre é reduzido, é uma lei natural. Isso também é viver! Gostaríamos de capturar apenas a alegria, mas é a sublime êxtase do amor que desencadeia a agonia mais atroz.

42. AME A SI MESMO

O Oráculo é um convite preciso: ame a si mesmo. De fato, o verdadeiro problema é que você nem se aceita!

Quantas vezes você fez o que lhe deu um verdadeiro prazer? Comece agora, aqui, imediatamente!

43. A CORAGEM DO AMOR

O próprio Oráculo é indefinido: é um aviso simples. Se você se enrijecer na rejeição, a força do amor será prejudicada. Por outro lado, se essa força assume em você o senso de coragem - seja para amar ou para aceitar o amor - então...

44. O ENCONTRO ÍNTIMO

O Oráculo é um aviso: se um encontro tão íntimo e profundo estiver vinculado a uma simples sedução - do homem ou da mulher -, ocorrerá uma catástrofe.

45. FELICIDADE É AMAR

Além da simples realidade do casal, o Oráculo fala de sucesso, quando se estende a dimensão do amor a um instrumento de coesão com o consórcio humano. Fazer isso é simples: basta amar

46. O SEXO

No início da união, o amor é sexualidade. Para evoluir, devemos nos abandonar ao jogo mais simples do amor: este é o convite do Oráculo.

47. A FALÊNCIA

Toda paixão se esgota... mas a interpretação é delicada; não deve ser lida de maneira negativa: o que está acontecendo faz parte do ciclo da vida. Você se sente vazio, carente? Não é *uma coisa ruim*, ao contrário, agora está na hora de voltar para si mesmo: a estação da solidão está se aproximando. Aprenda a dançar entre encontros e separações.

48. A FONTE

A imagem mostra o que há de mais profundo nos seres humanos: evoca nossa natureza essencial. O Oráculo é simples: não perca o contato com aquela interioridade íntima, porque é a partir daí que, conscientemente ou não, a força da vida que anima todos os seus gestos surge, por toda a sua vida.

49. O TÚMULO DO AMOR

No casamento, há uma repressão, uma domesticação do amor em função de outros interesses, dos principais medos do ego, que marcam seu fim. O Oráculo indica que é hora da revolução: avalie em que sua vida se baseia. O convite é se regenerar: em você existe uma força criativa capaz de renovar e renová-lo perpetuamente.

50. O CADINHO

O Oráculo é um convite para enraizar seu amor na dimensão da honestidade e sinceridade: você pode fazer isso, usando a sua energia para não depender do parceiro para sua sobrevivência... em todos os níveis!

51. O EVENTO FATAL

O conselho do Oráculo é viver esse momento de intensidade como ele é: deixará um rastro íntimo e perene em sua vida. Vá fundo no momento presente: sinta-se tremer, ouça esse arrepio, deixe o coração falar com ele. Isso acontece... só precisamos eliminar todos os obstáculos para que isso aconteça. Só então o amor continuará a recriar-se.

52. A TESTEMUNHA

Se você está em um estado de turbulência, se o amor está perturbando você com seu turbilhão... crie em você um espaço de quietude para fazer uma pausa!

53. A INTIMIDADE

A dimensão na qual o Oráculo fala não é a esfera da segurança, da posse e do ciúme. A intimidade, que é a montanha invisível do amor, tem suas bases em algo que não pode ser apreendido por nenhum dos cinco sentidos. Não passa de vazio e silêncio.

54. A JOVEM NOIVA

Todas as relações livres entre seres humanos estão descritas aqui. Para o I Ching a força do amor é tal que rompe e elimina todas as convenções e regras estabelecidas pelas normas sociais. O Oráculo fala da harmonia superior que o amor induz no mundo.

55. A PLENITUDE

Para o Oráculo, este é um momento de plenitude: o fogo ardente da força vital irrompe com o som do trovão, anulando-se e anulando toda inibição da consciência. Qualquer sensação de apatia desapareceu: você está enfrentando uma experiência vital. Talvez você a perceba como uma morte do ego, mas não precisa ter medo: pela primeira vez... você está vivendo!

56. O VIAJANTE

O presságio fala com o viajante o que existe em você. Ao passar de uma experiência para outra, ao encontrar amigos e amantes, você é um viajante. Algo impede que você pare para sempre: você tenta e tenta novamente, e toda as vezes parece que você atingiu um lar estável. Mas chega um momento, e é isso, em que você sente que deve retomar sua jornada.

57. O VENTO

O Oráculo nos convida a olhar para a existência: tudo o que acontece com você, qualquer coisa, observe-o *diretamente*... como simples fatos, sem julgar, sem dizer certo ou errado, bom ou ruim. Deixe a mente e seu julgamento perene de lado.

58. A AMIZADE

É uma comunicação fluida entre dois seres que se interpenetram... sem penetrarem-se! O Oráculo indica que, apesar de você, graças à intimidade, o relacionamento que você tem com seu parceiro se transformou em amizade.

59. A SOLIDÃO

O Oráculo nos convida a mergulhar completamente em nosso ser. Esta carta marca o fim de muitas experiências no mundo externo e indica o caminho a seguir para concluir uma evolução adicional. No auge de tantas experiências, o egoísmo dissolvido - a ideia de ser um pequeno eu separado e lutando contra tudo e contra todos - nos encontramos sozinhos. Na união íntima que é a essência da vida, nós ficamos sozinhos!

60. A LIMITAÇÃO

O hexagrama adverte: quando impomos limites muito severos ao amor isso impede a sua liberdade e o seu fluxo livre, dificultando sua evolução perene.

61. O MOMENTO PRESENTE

O hexagrama oferece a imagem de um coração livre, capaz de perceber o Verdadeiro e recebê-lo dentro de si. O Oráculo é um convite para mergulhar na verdade presente: viver aqui e agora *"quieora "* - em tempo real, onde habita toda a existência!

62. AS IDENTIFICAÇÕES

O Oráculo adverte: cuidado com as identificações! Certamente, o amor dá uma plenitude e uma beatitude incomparável, mas se alguém identifica essa plenitude com uma pessoa, abrimo-nos a espaços de imensa dor e desastre, constringindo nós mesmos e outra pessoa a uma escravidão ou dependência muito pesada.

63. A TRANSFIGURAÇÃO

Tudo chega à plenitude, em resolução completa, transfigura e coloca em contato com a dimensão do espírito... é um momento que esconde em si os sinais da decadência. Mergulhe e viva o máximo que puder nesta dimensão, antes que ela se torne uma memória, uma ilusão, um sonho.

64. A UNIÃO MÍSTICA

O Oráculo fala de um encontro perdido; cobiça-se algo, fica-se esperando, mas a fusão não acontece. É um aviso: na comunhão íntima gerada pelo amor com um amante, é possível apreender o possível *União mística* que é conclusão e realização. É um lampejo de intuição preciosa, mas inefável - por isso é essencial combinar amor com meditação.

И-ЦЗИН ЛЮБВИ

УПРОЩЕННЫЙ МЕТОД ПРОЧТЕНИЯ

Найдите момент, чтобы остаться наедине с собой, вдали от внешних волнений. Расслабьтесь, просто наблюдая за собственным дыханием, и лишь когда почувствуете, что соприкоснулись с наиболее сокровенной частью себя, смешайте карты: шестьдесят четыре гексаграммы, переведенные в образы, которые проанализировали ваше отношение к любви. Внутренне визуализируйте свою текущую ситуацию в любовной сфере. Позвольте ей предстать перед вами такой, какая она есть, не осуждайте ее, не интерпретируйте и не желайте изменений. Нет необходимости озвучивать ваш вопрос. Помните: вы не ищите утешения и не хотите изменить то, что происходит. Вы хотите понять. Когда почувствуете, что готовы начать, разложите перед собой колоду и левой рукой переверните одну карту. Прочитайте описание и рассмотрите изображение, думая о том, как оно проливает свет на вашу ситуацию. Закройте глаза и молча размышляйте над полученным посланием. Принятие является первым ключом к прочтению, так как оно способно произвести изменение. Но, прежде всего, оно способно помочь вам увидеть со стороны то, что жизнь предлагает вам… и помните: это тоже пройдет, это всего лишь один из периодов вашей жизни. А пока примите приглашение карты, без сопротивления и без волнений. Это основной урок И-Цзин Любви.

ПОСЛАНИЯ

1. ТВОРЧЕСКОЕ ЖЕЛАНИЕ
Восточная традиция полагает, что Вселенная родилась из желания. Эта карта призывает не усложнять вашу жизнь: примите желание. Не нужно бороться с сексуальностью. Каждый раз, подавляя себя, вы все больше боретесь с собой… и для полной реализации вам потребуются все ваши силы. Карта говорит о том, что вы находитесь в полной гармонии с творческой силой Вселенной.

2. ВОСПРИИМЧИВОСТЬ
Эта карта является признаком сильного присутствия Инь, то есть восприимчивости в вашей жизни. Понаблюдайте за тем, как Инь управляет вами, что подразумевает и что из этого вытекает: в вас творческая сила успокаивается и приобретает конкретность.

3. НАЧАЛЬНАЯ СЛОЖНОСТЬ

Оракул предлагает вам не превращать другого в объект использования или продавать себя во имя любви, но, скорее, предаться космическому магнетизму, который активизируется в любви.

4. НЕОПЫТНОСТЬ МОЛОДОСТИ

Оракул говорит, что вы стоите перед пропастью, но не беспокойтесь: по необходимости, небрежность, которая характеризует данную карту, приводит вас в движение. Таким образом, вы преодолеваете любое препятствие, которое мешает развиваться.

5. ОЖИДАНИЕ

В любовных ситуациях важно не мешать любви. Ожидание – это заклинание… На мгновение вы вступаете в контакт со своей собственной сущностью и приобретаете целостность. Оракул говорит, что вы в ожидании. Больше ничего не хочу!

6. КОНФЛИКТ

Мы обычно окрашиваем любовь мечтами и фантазиями, претензиями и убеждениями, не позволяя им существовать или оправдывая их до такой степени, что они деформируются. Это ваш случай? Посмотрите, как вы манипулируете своей любовью.

7. СПЛОЧЕННОСТЬ

В любой жизненной ситуации, и, прежде всего, в любви, хорошо иметь точку опоры на сплоченности. Разделяя любую встречу с другими, вы сможете обогатиться подобными контактами. Переориентируйте себя!

8. СОГЛАСОВАННОСТЬ ПОЛОВИНОК

Дао, чтобы проявить себя, удваивается. Именно чередование покоя и движения создает жизнь: игру причин и следствий, за которой что-то остается вечно неподвижным. Мудрость в том, чтобы ощутить в себе присутствующую в нас точку абсолютной неподвижности: глаз бури.

9. БЕССИЛИЕ

Вы перегружены событиями, но ничего не можете сделать, чтобы ситуация двигалась. Вы не можете вызвать никаких изменений. Примите эту беспомощность. Это тоже любовь.

10. ВАШЕ ВНУТРЕННЕЕ РУКОВОДСТВО

Оракул напоминает, что внутри вас есть руководство, которое может привести вас к счастью. Но вы им не пользуетесь. Вы даже не знаете об этом! Не волнуйтесь: его можно оживить, его нужно разбудить, если хотите жить в полноте любви.

11. ГАРМОНИЯ: ЛЮБОВЬ И МИР

Сливаясь с переживанием любви, вы погружаетесь в полноту настоящего момента: в нем есть полное исполнение. Позвольте потерять себя в краткости этого момента, в объятиях любимого человека. Не просите большего!

12. ПОВЕРХНОСТЬ

Давайте не будем обманывать себя: мы любим по самым разным причинам и все они приходят к стагнации. И-Цзин советует погрузиться в себя, в свою тайную близость, придать любви глубину.

13. БЫТЬ ВЛЮБЛЕННЫМ

Любая любовь несет в себе идею открытости, которая не навязывает свою волю, а, скорее, передает смысл и вибрацию гармонии с универсальной силой. Эта сила управляет всем существованием. Любовь – это сила сама по себе, она не навязывает себя: она ограничена необходимостью делиться.

14. СОВОКУПНОСТЬ

Времена благоприятны: у вас есть мудрость жизни, которая дарует полную свободу действий. И тот факт, что это не эгоизм, проявится в том, что вы ничего не делаете для достижения этой гармонии.

15. УНИКАЛЬНОСТЬ

Любовь случается, и в этом нет ничего особенного: в скромном образе, который иллюстрирует гексаграмма, видна «гора на заднем плане», которая прячется за «холмом на переднем плане». Данная карта – благоприятное предзнаменование.

16. РВЕНИЕ

Оракул свидетельствует о счастливом порыве силы, который, когда он разделен с другим, становится пылким. Успех приходит от самоотдачи в любви: единственное, что нужно, это отсутствие сопротивления.

17. СЛЕДИ ЗА СОБОЙ

Оракул говорит о том, что происходит при взгляде на самого себя. Смысл прост: принять положение вещей. В этой гармонии, которая не является ни снисходительной, ни компромиссной, человек участвует в естественном ритме мира.

18. ОСОЗНАНИЕ

Гексаграмма изображает неподвижную ситуацию. Оракул не хочет судить о подобном состоянии вещей, но предлагает подумать о механизмах и условиях, которые его создают. Необходимо сосредоточиться на внутренних качествах, чтобы найти выход из ситуации застоя, в которой мы можем только гнить.

19. СЛУШАТЬ ДРУГ ДРУГА

Оракул предупреждает о процветании. Вы развиваетесь в ситуации, которая день за днем созревает и приносит плоды.

20. СОЗЕРЦАНИЕ

В целом, в доктрине даосизма, эта гексаграмма представляет мировоззрение мудреца: Куан – это внимание без объекта, неограниченное Эго. На практике это медитация… другая сторона любви: учитесь включать ее в свою повседневную жизнь.

21. ПРЕДАТЕЛЬСТВО (РЕВНОСТЬ)

Вы испытываете темную сторону любви? Дайте себе время ассимилировать предательство. В эти отчаянные моменты то, что мы любим в другом человеке, проявляется с абсолютной ясностью: наблюдайте это и делайте это своим, сохраняя свою совесть внутри себя. В этом внимательном присутствии необходимо расти и развиваться. Станьте собой!

22. КАСАНИЕ

Кажется, что карта благоприятна. На мгновение вы обнаружите, что живете в пространстве, свободном от каких-либо беспокойств… оно течет против вашей воли. Однако Оракул предупреждает: поскольку все это вызвано чем-то внешним для вас, оно неизбежно зависит от внешнего стимула, поэтому и нестабильно.

23. ИЗНОС ВРЕМЕНИ

Любовь открывается чему-то вечному, но поскольку она рождается во времени, ей суждено погибнуть, несмотря на благие намерения. Оракул указывает на принятие: он остается устойчивым, как гора, сохраняет абсолютную неподвижность и позволяет пережить то, что с вами происходит. Это тоже пройдет.

24. НОВОЕ НАЧАЛО

Вы сталкиваетесь с новым началом. Попробуйте спросить себя: «Где истинный источник света, который я называю любовью?». Таким образом, благодаря импульсу любви, вы приблизитесь к своему внутреннему центру и увидите свое изначальное лицо: это сокровенное и глубокое пламя, которое обитает в глубине вашего существа.

25. НЕВИННОСТЬ РЕБЕНКА

Гексаграмма приводит к естественному положению вещей. Это приглашение действовать как ребенок: это настоящее безупречное поведение.

26. СТРАХ ЛЮБВИ

Оракул указывает, что вы наслаждаетесь значительной силой, поэтому сейчас самое время для прогресса. Наберитесь смелости из своего нынешнего состояния власти, чтобы полностью отказаться от себя… не уходите! Из-за страха многие не смеют любить, довольствуясь приятными компромиссами.

27. ПИТАНИЕ

Это правильный способ измерять любовь: драгоценное питание, а не еда, и Оракул советует не упустить его, если вы хотите поддерживать здоровый психофизический баланс.

28. ПОД ДАВЛЕНИЕМ

Ситуация очень серьезная: трудности кажутся непреодолимыми. Положение, в котором вы находитесь, отчаянное, если не сказать больше. Как из него выбраться? Сохраняйте радостное спокойствие. Независимо от того, насколько серьезна опасность... выход в доверии, сейчас самое время сосредоточиться на своем бьющемся сердце.

29. ТЕМНАЯ НОЧЬ ДУШИ

Вы под воздействием, ощущая экзистенциальную тревогу, которая набрасывает тень на вашу жизнь. Оракул предлагает простой выход: нужно идти к сути событий, а не останавливаться на их поверхности. В этом смысле предзнаменование положительно: независимо от темноты, в которую вы погружены, в вас есть осознание, способное постичь данное учение. Остановитесь на нем!

30. ВЛЮБЛЕННОСТЬ

Гексаграмма воплощает «природу в ее великолепии», поэтому Оракул дает простой ответ: то, что вы испытываете, поднимает сердце и дух, и связывает вас с вечным и бессмертным великолепием любви. Пусть это пламя горит в полную силу. Не ожидайте ничего другого.

31. ПОМОЛВКА

Оракул говорит о союзе основополагающих сил, поэтому предзнаменование счастливое. Будьте восприимчивы к тому, что происходит глобально: отстранитесь от того, что происходит локально.

32. ДЛИТЕЛЬНОСТЬ

Оракул призывает избегать рутины. Погруженная в повседневную жизнь, любовь сразу умирает. Продолжительность характеризуется постоянным преобразованием и, следовательно, постоянным обновлением.

33. ОБМАН

Что-то обращает любовь в бегство. Фактически, эта энергия отступает, чтобы защитить себя: она не может поступить иначе. Короче говоря, вы будете измотаны и больше не увидите даже тени любви!

34. ДОВЕРИЕ

Гексаграмма указывает на власть силы, твердости. Поэтому Оракул говорит, что у вас есть возможность достичь истинного величия: нужно развиваться только естественным путем.

35. ИГРА В ЛЮБОВЬ

Предсказание благоприятно: оно говорит о расширении. В конце концов, вы поняли, что любовь – это игра… ничто в вас не мешает ей появиться.

36. ОДЕРЖИМОСТЬ (ЖАДНОСТЬ)

Свет любви затемняется природными или ментальными силами, которые вступили во владение. Его естественность задыхается или затемняется чем-то, что мешает его свободному выражению, как простой потребности души. Обратите внимание, как вы вмешиваетесь в ситуации, которые исказили ваше воображение и способность жить плавно.

37. СЕМЬЯ

Эта гексаграмма говорит о семье: это голос сына, который оплакивает судьбу своей матери, или нежные ограничения, которые проявляются в колоссальном усилии в воспитании неблагодарных детей. Оракул призывает увидеть значение вашей глубокой любви в семье.

38. «НЕТ» В ЛЮБВИ

Это неразделенная любовь. Оракул говорит о нескончаемом разнообразии, разобщенности и сепарации. Две воли в игре выражают себя и не встречаются, они не гармонируют.

39. ПРЕПЯТСТВИЕ
Рядом с непреодолимой вершиной пролегает страшная бездна. Кажется, выхода нет: опасность парализует. Нам нужно найти способ обойти эти препятствия. Что делать? Настало время для медитации и осознания.

40. ОСВОБОЖДЕНИЕ
Оракул указывает на истинное, настоящее освобождение, отличное от общего толкования данного слова: это не отрицание желания, но и не его достижение. Это отстраненное и нейтральное созерцание.

41. СТРАДАНИЕ
Шаг за шагом каждое удовольствие сгущается, застывает, превращается в камень. Радостный импульс истощается, это естественный закон. Это тоже жизнь! Мы хотели бы наблюдать только радость, но именно возвышенный экстаз любви вызывает самую жестокую агонию.

42. ЛЮБИТЬ САМОГО СЕБЯ
Оракул призывает с ясностью: люби самого себя. На самом деле, настоящая проблема в том, что вы часто даже не принимаете себя! Сколько раз вы делали то, что доставляло вам истинное удовольствие? Начните немедленно, здесь и сейчас!

43. СМЕЛОСТЬ ЛЮБВИ

Сам Оракул не определен: это простое предупреждение. Если вы будете стараться отвергнуть любовь, сила любви будет ограничена. И наоборот, если эта сила требует от вас мужества любить или принимать любовь, тогда…

44. ИНТИМНАЯ ВСТРЕЧА

Оракул предупреждает: если близкая интимная встреча вызвана простым соблазнением мужчины или женщины, то произойдет катастрофа.

45. СЧАСТЬЕ – ЭТО ЛЮБИТЬ

Помимо простой ситуации одной пары, Оракул говорит об успехе, когда любовь используется, как инструмент сплоченности в человеческом обществе. Делать это легко: достаточно любить.

46. СЕКС

В начале союза любви – это сексуальность. Оракул советует: чтобы развиваться, мы должны отказаться от самой простой игры в любовь.

47. НЕУДАЧА

Вся страсть исчерпана,… но интерпретация деликатна; ее не следует воспринимать негативно: происходящее является частью жизненного цикла. Вы чувствуете себя опустошенным? Это не плохо, наоборот, теперь пришло время вернуться к себе: приближается сезон одиночества. Научитесь вальсировать между встречами и расставаниями.

48. ИСТОЧНИК

Изображение рисует то, что находится глубоко в нас, людях: оно пробуждает нашу сущностную природу. Оракул дает простой совет: не теряйте контакта с этим внутренним пространством, потому что именно оттуда – сознательно или нет – возникает жизненная сила, которая оживляет каждый наш жест, всю нашу жизнь.

49. МОГИЛА ЛЮБВИ

В браке происходит подавление, «одомашнивание» любви в зависимости от других интересов, первичных страхов Эго, которые грозят ей смертью. Оракул предупреждает, что настало время для революции: оцените, на чем основана ваша жизнь. Совет – возродите себя: в вас есть творческая сила, способная постоянно обновлять себя и все вокруг.

50. ЗАКАЛКА

Оракул предлагает укоренить вашу любовь в аспекте честности и искренности: можете сделать это, используя свою энергию, чтобы не зависеть от партнера в собственном выживании… на всех уровнях!

51. РОКОВОЕ СОБЫТИЕ

Совет Оракула состоит в том, чтобы прожить этот момент напряженности таким, какой он есть: он оставит интимный и вечный след в вашей жизни. Войдите глубоко в настоящий момент: почувствуйте себя дрожащим, прислушайтесь к этой дрожи, позвольте сердцу поговорить с самим собой. Это случается... нам просто нужно устранить все препятствия, чтобы это произошло. Только так любовь может воссоздавать себя.

52. СВИДЕТЕЛЬ

Если вы находитесь в состоянии суматохи, если любовь расстраивает вас своим кружением... создайте внутри себя пространство неподвижности, в котором можно остановиться!

53. ИНТИМНОСТЬ

Измерение, о котором говорит Оракул, не является сферой безопасности, одержимости и ревности. Близость, которая является невидимой горой любви, коренится в том, что невозможно понять на основе пяти чувств. Это не что иное, как пустота и тишина.

54. МОЛОДАЯ НЕВЕСТА

Здесь изображены все свободные отношения между людьми. Для И-Цзин сила любви такова, что она разрушает и уничтожает все правила и условности, установленные социальными нормами. Оракул говорит о высшей гармонии, которую любовь дарит миру.

55. НАПОЛНЕННОСТЬ

Для Оракула это момент наполненности: пылающий огонь жизненной силы разряжается звуком грома, исчезая и уничтожая всякое угрызение совести. Любое чувство апатии исчезло: вы сталкиваетесь с жизненным опытом. Возможно, вы воспринимаете это как смерть Эго, но не нужно бояться: впервые… вы живете!

56. ПУТЕШЕСТВЕННИК

Предзнаменование обращено к сокрытому внутри вас путешественнику. Переходя от одного опыта к другому, встречаясь с друзьями и любовниками, вы становитесь путником. Что-то мешает вам окончательно остановиться: вы пытаетесь пробовать снова, и каждый раз, кажется, достигаете стабильной гавани. Но наступает время, когда вы чувствуете, что должны возобновить свое путешествие.

57. ВЕТЕР

Оракул предлагает вам взглянуть на ваше существование, на все, что происходит с вами. Смотрите на все прямо… как на простые факты, без ярлыков, без правильных или неправильных, хороших или плохих определений. Оставьте ум и его извечное стремление судить в стороне.

8. ДРУЖБА

Это текучая связь между двумя существами, которые проникают… не проникая! Оракул говорит о том, что, несмотря на ваше участие, благодаря близости, ваши отношения с партнером превратились в дружбу.

59. ОДИНОЧЕСТВО

Оракул приглашает вас полностью погрузиться в свое существование. Эта карта отмечает окончание многих опытов во внешнем мире и указывает путь, которым нужно следовать, чтобы завершить дальнейшую эволюцию. На пике стольких переживаний эгоизм растворился. Это намек на то, чтобы быть маленьким отдельным «Я», которое борется против всего и всех. Так мы оказываемся в одиночестве. В интимном союзе, который является сутью жизни, человек одинок!

60. ОГРАНИЧЕНИЕ

Гексаграмма предупреждает: накладывая слишком строгие ограничения на любовь, мы препятствуем свободному течению, останавливая ее вечное развитие.

61. НАСТОЯЩИЙ МОМЕНТ

Гексаграмма олицетворяет образ свободного сердца, способного воспринимать Истину и приветствовать ее внутри себя. Оракул – это приглашение погрузиться в собственную настоящую истину: живите спокойно в реальном времени, где коренится все бытие!

62. ИДЕНТИФИКАЦИЯ

Оракул предупреждает: остерегайтесь идентифика́ций! Конечно, любовь дарит полноту и несравненное блаженство, но если отождествить эту полноту с человеком, он может стать сосредоточением огромной боли и бедствия, заставляя себя и партнера испытывать тяжкое рабство или зависимость.

63. ПРЕОБРАЖЕНИЕ

Все достигает полноты, разрешения, преображения, все соприкасается с изменением духа… это момент, который скрывает в себе признаки упадка. Погрузитесь в себя и живите как можно дольше в этом измерении, пока оно не станет воспоминанием, иллюзией, мечтой.

64. МИСТИЧЕСКИЙ СОЮЗ

Оракул говорит о пропущенной встрече; он надеется на что-то, но слияние не наступает. Это предупреждение: в близком общении, порожденном любовью с партнером, мы начинаем понимать возможный мистический союз, который является завершением и реализацией. Это вспышка драгоценной, но невыразимой интуиции – для этого необходимо сочетать любовь с медитацией.